Contents

Introduction

'As I write, highly civilised human beings are flying overhead, trying to kill me.'

George Orwell, 'England Your England', 1941

In the twentieth century, the world was plunged into a chaotic whirlwind of violence, prejudice and fear. It was an era that saw death and destruction on a scale not previously even imagined. In many ways, this is a book about conflict – full of wars, revolutions and bitter hatreds between opposed groups of people.

The First World War was the original catastrophe: it created upheaval throughout Europe and led to the rise of brutal dictators all across the continent. These dictators then pushed the surviving democracies into a second and even greater world war.

Following the Second World War, the people of the colonies in Asia and Africa fought to win independence from their European rulers. In what became the dominant nation in the world, the United States of America, there was a long struggle for justice before all its citizens could win equal rights. And even when the World Wars were over, the international rivalry of the Cold War threatened to bring about still greater horrors, through the power of the nuclear bomb.

One word that is missing from the title of this book, and that makes it different from the previous volumes in this series, is 'Britain'. This is still a textbook for British students, and there remains some focus on British history. But in the twentieth century, the events that most affected Britain usually did not take place in this country. We must look to Europe, and sometimes to the world beyond, in order to understand Britain's place within our most recent history.

Robert Selth

Collins

Key Stage 3

Twentieth Century World

Robert Selth

William Collins' dream of knowledge for all began with the publication of his first book in 1819. A self-educated mill worker, he not only enriched millions of lives, but also founded a flourishing publishing house. Today, staying true to this spirit, Collins books are packed with inspiration, innovation and practical expertise. They place you at the centre of a world of possibility and give you exactly what you need to explore it.

Collins. Freedom to teach.

Published by Collins
An imprint of HarperCollins*Publishers*
The News Building
1 London Bridge Street
London
SE1 9GF

Browse the complete Collins catalogue at
www.collins.co.uk

British Library Cataloguing-in-Publication Data
A catalogue record for this publication is available from the British Library.

Author: Robert Selth
Publisher: Katie Sergeant
Product manager: Caroline Green
Editorial assistant: Tina Pietron
Reviewer: Robert Peal
Copyeditor: Hugh Hillyard-Parker
Fact checker: Barbara Hibbard
Proof readers: Catherine Dakin and Claire Throp
Maps: © Collins Bartholomew Limited 2019
Indexer: Lisa Footitt
Picture researchers: Caroline Green and Tina Pietron
Text permissions researcher: Rachel Thorne
Cover and internal typesetter: Ken Vail Graphic Design
Cover photograph: TroobaDoor/Shutterstock
Production controller: Katherine Willard
Printed and bound by CPI Group (UK) Ltd, Croydon, CRO 4YY

Concise chapter introductions set the scene for each topic.

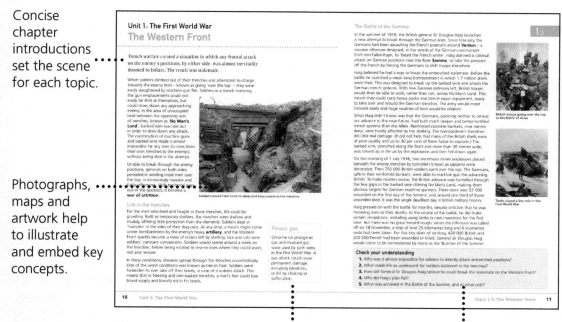

Photographs, maps and artwork help to illustrate and embed key concepts.

Fact boxes provide interesting, bite-sized information and details.

Check your understanding questions at the end of every chapter allow you to check and consolidate your learning.

Knowledge organisers can be used to revise and quiz yourself on key dates, people and definitions.

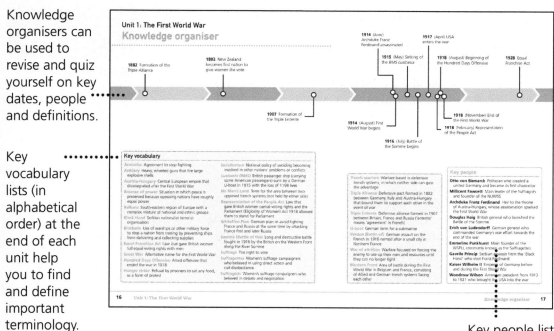

Key vocabulary lists (in alphabetical order) at the end of each unit help you to find and define important terminology.

Key people lists (in alphabetical order) recap the people of influence covered in each unit.

Unit 1: The First World War
Europe in 1914

In the early twentieth century, the five great powers of Europe – Britain, Austria-Hungary, Germany, France and Russia – existed in a balance of power, but tension was growing between them.

In the nineteenth century, Europe had been broadly peaceful, stable and prosperous. Though there had been several smaller conflicts, the continent had not known large-scale warfare since Napoleon's defeat at Waterloo in 1815. However, by 1914 diplomats were struggling to prevent a range of international rivalries and disputes from developing into war.

Germany

In the 1860s, a powerful new nation had appeared in central Europe. Otto von Bismarck was the ambitious Prime Minister of Prussia, the most powerful of the German-speaking kingdoms. He brought together the dozens of small states in the region to craft a new, united nation: Germany.

Otto von Bismarck (1815–1898)

Bismarck understood that the older powers of Europe would fear and mistrust the new country. Germany possessed important industrial areas and commanded a large, well-disciplined army. Bismarck therefore worked tirelessly to build and preserve friendly relationships with Germany's neighbours. He forged the **Triple Alliance** – a defensive pact between Germany, Italy and Austria-Hungary that bound them to support each other in the event of war – and successfully kept Germany on good terms with Russia and France. Bismarck's successors, however, were less careful to protect the peace. Following his retirement in 1890, a series of chancellors enlarged the German army, provoking suspicion throughout Europe. To make matters worse, from 1888 Germany's emperor was Kaiser Wilhelm II, who regularly made tactless public comments about the inevitability of war.

France and Russia

In the process of German unification, France had been defeated in a short but decisive conflict, the Franco-Prussian War of 1870–71. Ever since, the French had longed to restore their national honour and recover the two provinces that Germany had annexed, Alsace and Lorraine.

France's key ally, Russia, had no particular quarrel with Germany. However, in the years before 1914 Russia was modernising its military by increasing recruitment, improving its large army, and extending its railway network. Observing these reforms, German military planners calculated that Germany would not be able to win a war with Russia after 1916. Senior German officers advised their government that any war with Russia had better come sooner rather than later.

Britain

The traditional foreign policy of Britain was to avoid close involvement in European affairs, focusing instead on the global British Empire. British politicians were nonetheless disturbed by the economic growth of Germany, which had come to control a huge share of international trade. In particular, Germany's attempts to enlarge and modernise its navy raised fears that Germany might soon challenge British supremacy at sea.

Anti-German attitudes in Britain were one factor in the creation of the **Triple Entente**, a defensive military alliance formed in 1907 between Britain, Russia and France ('entente' is French for 'agreement'). For the previous hundred years, France and Russia had been Britain's major imperial rivals, both competing with Britain for global territory – unlike Germany, which had few colonies. However, security in Europe proved more important than contests for land in Africa or Asia.

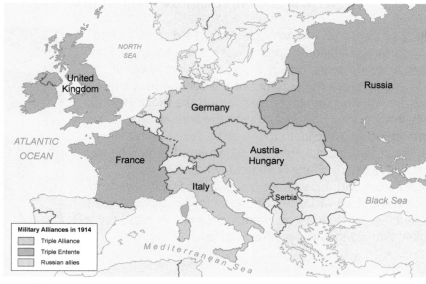

Map of Europe, 1914

Austria-Hungary

Germany's one dependable ally among the great powers was the Austro-Hungarian empire. This was an empire of different national and linguistic groups, ruled by the Austrian emperor in Vienna. In the south, the empire stretched into the **Balkans**, an unstable region of south-east Europe with a mixture of national and ethnic groups. Within the Balkans was the small, independent nation of Serbia. Many Serbs lived within the southern parts of the Austro-Hungarian empire, and the key foreign policy of independent Serbia was to eventually 'liberate' them, expanding Serbian territory. The Serbs therefore took every opportunity to destabilise the empire to their north.

Complicating the situation was Russia, an ally of Serbia. Pan-Slavism, the belief that ethnically Slavic people should support each other, was popular in Russia and was used to justify close Russian involvement in Serbian politics.

Check your understanding

1. Why were the other great powers of Europe suspicious of Germany?
2. Why was there widespread desire in France for a war with Germany?
3. Why did German military planners believe that if there was going to be war, it would be better sooner rather than later?
4. Why was the Triple Entente formed in 1907?
5. Why was Serbia a problem for the Austro-Hungarian empire?

Unit 1: The First World War
The outbreak of war

In an atmosphere of hostility and uncertainty, an isolated crisis in Bosnia triggered a chain of responses that resulted in war.

On 28 June 1914, the Archduke Franz Ferdinand, heir to the throne of Austria-Hungary, was visiting Sarajevo. This was a city in Bosnia, one of the southern provinces of the empire and a major target of the Serbian nationalist movement. The Serbian terrorist group the **Black Hand**, which was closely connected with the Serbian army, attempted to assassinate the Archduke. The bomb they threw at the Archduke's motorcade injured several people but did not harm Franz Ferdinand, who insisted on proceeding with his visit. However, while Franz Ferdinand was being driven to the city hospital to visit the wounded, a nineteen-year-old assassin named Gavrilo Princip shot and killed him along with his wife, Sophie.

Archduke Franz Ferdinand and his wife, Sophie, on the day they were assassinated

The July crisis

The Austro-Hungarian government responded with shock and fury to the assassinations. It was immediately decided that they should invade Serbia as punishment for the attack and in order to neutralise the Serbian threat once and for all. On 23 July, Austria-Hungary presented Serbia with an ultimatum demanding that Serbia meet a series of demands or face war. Serbia refused, and on 28 July, Austria-Hungary declared war.

Russia was bound to defend Serbia, and so on 30 July, Russia became the first of the great powers to mobilise its army for war. Germany, desperately seeking to prevent the war from spreading beyond the Austro-Serbian conflict, requested that Russia cease mobilisation within twelve hours. When Russia ignored this request, Germany declared war and immediately mobilised its armies against Russia – and also, in accordance with the Schlieffen Plan, against France.

In order to attack France at the most convenient point, Germany chose to march its army through neutral Belgium. Troops entered Belgium on 4 August and faced immediate resistance from the Belgian army, as Belgium refused to let German troops cross its territory. The violation of Belgian neutrality encouraged Britain to intervene, and so on 4 August, Britain declared war on Germany.

With the intervention of Britain, all five of the great powers were engaged, and Europe was at war. Britain, France and Russia became known as the Allies, while Germany and Austria-Hungary were called the Central Powers. Italy did not honour the Triple Alliance, abandoning its commitments to Germany and Austria-Hungary, and joined the war on the side of the Allies in 1915.

The Schlieffen Plan

German war planning was based on the **Schlieffen Plan**, designed to avoid Germany having to divide its strength to fight both France and Russia at the same time. Under this plan, Germany would begin with a massive strike against France, allowing it to defeat France within six weeks. Then it would shift most of its armies eastwards to confront Russia. Thus, when war came, Germany's first priority was to attack France as quickly and forcefully as possible.

The beginning of trench warfare

It was commonly assumed that the **Great War** (as it soon became known) would be over by Christmas. Only a handful of far-sighted commanders, including the British war minister Lord Kitchener, predicted that it might last for years. The chief reason the war went on for so long was that it soon degenerated into a new and seemingly unwinnable form of combat: **trench warfare**.

For its first few months, the war was fought as a conventional 'war of movement', with mobile armies confronting each other in traditional battles. The Germans advanced far into France, almost reaching Paris, but were stopped in early September at the Battle of the Marne. After the Germans had withdrawn slightly to a line north of the River Aisne, neither side could advance; instead, they both began moving northward in order to outflank one another. This developed into a 'race to the sea' that ended only when both armies had reached the English Channel in late October. As winter drew in, the Germans and the Allies faced each other along a 700-kilometre line, stretching right across France from the Channel to the border with Switzerland.

Accepting that they could launch no more offensives until the spring, the armies dug systems of fortified trenches that could house soldiers indefinitely and could be defended with machine guns against any attack. The result was a pair of opposed, immobile defensive systems. This was the **Western Front**. In eastern Europe, a similar process occurred: despite a German victory at Tannenberg in August, neither the Central Powers nor the Russians could secure an advantage, and on much of the front they were forced to resort to digging trenches. On both the Western Front and Eastern Front, the war became a static one, in which armies occupied the same positions, fighting from the same trenches, for years on end.

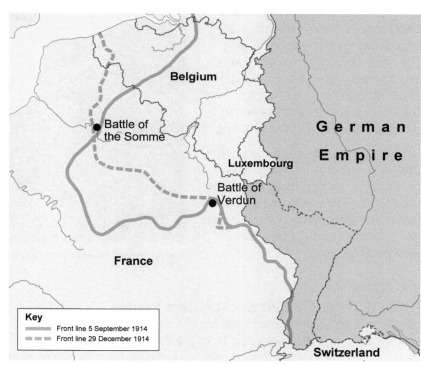

Map showing the Western Front, 1914, with 1916 battle sites

Check your understanding

1. Why was the Archduke Franz Ferdinand assassinated on 28 June 1914?
2. What did Austria-Hungary do in response to the assassination of Franz Ferdinand?
3. What was the German war strategy laid out in the Schlieffen Plan?
4. What German action provoked Britain to enter the war?
5. What was the Western Front?

Unit 1: The First World War
The Western Front

Trench warfare created a situation in which any frontal attack on the enemy's positions, by either side, was almost inevitably doomed to failure. The result was stalemate.

When soldiers climbed out of their trenches and attempted to charge towards the enemy lines – known as going 'over the top' – they were easily slaughtered by machine gun fire. Soldiers in a trench manning the gun emplacements could not easily be shot at themselves, but could mow down any approaching enemy. In the area of unoccupied land between the opposing sets of trenches, known as '**No Man's Land**', barbed wire was laid out in order to slow down any attack. The combination of machine guns and barbed wire made it almost impossible for any men to cross from their own trenches to the enemy's without being shot in the attempt.

Unable to break through the enemy positions, generals on both sides persisted in sending more men over the top, in increasingly massive and futile offensives. With territorial gain out of the question, it became a **war of attrition**.

Soldiers would take turns to sleep and keep watch in the trenches

Life in the trenches

For the men who lived and fought in these trenches, life could be gruelling. Built as temporary shelters, the trenches were shallow and muddy, offering little protection from the elements. Soldiers slept in 'foxholes' in the sides of their dug-outs. At any time, a trench might come under bombardment by the enemy's heavy **artillery**, and the Western Front quickly became a mass of craters left by shelling. Lice and rats were soldiers' constant companions. Soldiers would spend around a week on the frontline, before being rotated to reserve lines where they could wash, rest and recover.

In these conditions, diseases spread through the trenches uncontrollably. One of the worst conditions was known as trench foot. Soldiers were forbidden to ever take off their boots, in case of a sudden attack. This meant that in freezing and rain-soaked trenches, a man's feet could lose blood supply and literally rot in his boots.

Poison gas

Chlorine (or phosgene) gas and mustard gas were used by both sides in the First World War. A gas attack could cause permanent damage, including blindness, or kill by choking or suffocation.

The Battle of the Somme

In the summer of 1916, the British general Sir Douglas Haig launched a new attempt to break through the German lines. Since February, the Germans had been assaulting the French positions around **Verdun** – a massive offensive designed, in the words of the German commander Erich von Falkenhayn, to 'bleed the French white'. Haig planned a colossal attack on German positions near the River **Somme**, to take the pressure off the French by forcing the Germans to shift troops elsewhere.

Haig believed he had a way to break the entrenched stalemate. Before the battle he launched a week-long bombardment in which 1.7 million shells were fired. This was designed to break up the barbed wire and smash the German trench systems. With few German defences left, British troops would then be able to walk, rather than run, across No Man's Land. This meant they could carry heavy packs and trench repair equipment, ready to take over and rebuild the German trenches. The army would move forward easily and huge swathes of land would be retaken.

British troops going over the top at the Battle of Arras

What Haig didn't know was that the Germans, planning neither to retreat nor advance in the near future, had built much deeper and better-fortified trench systems than the Allies. Reinforced concrete bunkers, nine metres deep, were hardly affected by the shelling. The bombardment therefore did little real damage. (It did not help that many of the British shells were of poor quality and up to 30 per cent of them failed to explode.) The barbed wire, stretched along the front and more than 30 metres wide, was tossed up in the air by the explosions and then fell down again.

On the morning of 1 July 1916, two enormous mines (explosives placed beneath the enemy trenches by tunnellers known as sappers) were detonated. Then 750 000 British soldiers went over the top. The Germans, safe in their reinforced bunkers, were able to machine gun the advancing British. To make matters worse, the British advance was funnelled through the few gaps in the barbed wire littering No Man's Land, making them obvious targets for German machine gunners. There were over 57 000 wounded on the first day of the Somme, and around one third of those wounded died. It was the single deadliest day in British military history.

Tanks played a key role in the First World War

Haig pressed on with the battle for months, despite criticism that he was throwing men to their deaths. In the course of the battle, he did make certain innovations, including using tanks (a new invention) for the first time. But there was no great breakthrough: when the offensive was called off on 18 November, a strip of land 25 kilometres long and 6 kilometres wide had been taken. For this tiny sliver of territory, 420 000 British and 200 000 French had been wounded or killed. General Sir Douglas Haig would come to be remembered by many as the 'Butcher of the Somme'.

Check your understanding

1. Why was it almost impossible for soldiers to directly attack entrenched positions?
2. What made life so unpleasant for soldiers stationed in the trenches?
3. How did General Sir Douglas Haig believe he could break the stalemate on the Western Front?
4. Why did Haig's plan fail?
5. What was achieved in the Battle of the Somme, and at what cost?

Unit 1: The First World War
Allied victory

By 1917, soldiers and civilians had lost faith in the war, and there was disillusionment on all sides. Yet in that year, the direction of the war would be permanently changed.

By 1917, Germany was suffering and struggling to continue fighting – but not because of events on the battlefield. Since the beginning of the conflict, the British had been using their navy to **blockade** Germany. This meant stopping and preventing ships carrying supplies from reaching German ports, thus starving German industry of the raw materials it needed. The blockade worked: German trade fell from $5.9 billion to $0.8 billion between 1914 and 1917, and German civilians were soon experiencing severe shortages of food and fuel.

Painting of *RMS Lusitania* torpedoed by a German submarine

In response to the blockade, German **U-boats** (submarines) launched attacks on Allied shipping. In 1915, the Germans declared 'unrestricted submarine warfare', which meant their U-boats could attack without warning and target civilian as well as military vessels – ignoring the conventional rules of naval combat. It was this U-boat campaign that would eventually tip the scales of the war decisively by bringing in a new and strong combatant on the Allied side.

America in, Russia out

On 7 May 1915, a German U-boat torpedoed and sank the British passenger liner *RMS Lusitania*. Among the 1198 people killed 128 were Americans, and the attack provoked outrage in the United States. Over the following years, American ships suspected of carrying supplies to Britain and France were also targeted. Eventually, in response to increasing popular pressure, President Woodrow Wilson brought America into the war on the side of the Allies on 6 April 1917. This was a major departure from the traditional American policy of **isolationism**: keeping out of the affairs of Europe.

American soldiers in a front line trench during the Meuse-Argonne Offensive

The Americans took many months to arrive in Europe in significant numbers, but the money they provided for supplies and armaments rejuvenated the Allied war effort. Within the same year, however, a second political change brought an unexpected change of fortunes for the Germans. Following the Bolshevik Revolution in October (see pages 18–19), Russia made peace with Germany and withdrew from the war. The Eastern Front was closed down, and large numbers of German troops could now be transferred to the west.

The final offensives

With German civilians starving, and with almost 300 000 American troops already in France, Germany needed a quick victory. Three years of attrition and blockade had left their troops exhausted, underequipped, and underfed, while newer recruits were badly trained and ill-disciplined. These men would be no match for the Americans. The renowned general Erich von Ludendorff, by now the leading figure in the German army, saw this clearly. Ludendorff therefore gambled on a final, massive offensive in the spring of 1918, designed to smash through France and win the war before the Americans could make too great a difference.

The Ludendorff Offensive, as it became known, was remarkably successful at first. This was because Ludendorff had devised new battlefield tactics that at last managed to break the stalemate on the Western Front. He used small bands of lightly equipped, fast-moving 'storm troops' to punch through the Allied line at weak points all along the front, rather than sending a massive wave of troops to attack a single point. This worked, and German soldiers poured through the gaps, managing to advance 64 kilometres. The Great War was briefly a war of movement again. But the offensive cost 400 000 men, and by this time, Germany was completely out of reserves. The advance outran their supply lines, and the Allies inevitably began to push back.

From 8 August, the Allies launched their own massive counterattack all along the Western Front. Known as the **Hundred Days Offensive**, this campaign relied on large numbers of new and well-trained troops, ample supplies and first-rate equipment – all thanks to American contributions. By October, the Germans were in full retreat, abandoning their trenches and pulling back out of France. Recognising defeat, Kaiser Wilhelm II abdicated on 9 November. Two days later, on 11 November 1918, the two sides signed an **armistice**, and the fighting at last came to an end.

Legacy

The First World War was the most brutal and destructive conflict the world had ever seen. It took the lives of between nine and eleven million soldiers, and around eight million civilians. It ended the confidence of nineteenth-century Europe in progress and improvement, giving rise to an age of uncertainty, violence and political upheaval across the continent. Finally, by pushing Russia into revolution and leaving Germany broken and humiliated, the war planted the seeds for the even greater and more terrible conflict that would soon engulf the world.

The end of Austria-Hungary

Under economic blockade along with the Germans, the people of the Austro-Hungarian empire had been starving for years. When it became clear that the Allies were going to win the war, they began pressing for independence. In the final few months of 1918, the empire's Balkan Slavic population (Serbs, Croats, and Slovenes) joined with independent Serbia to form the new state of Yugoslavia, while Poles, Hungarians and Czechs all declared their own states. With dramatic speed, the empire fell apart.

Check your understanding

1. What were the effects of the British naval blockade of Germany?

2. Why did the United States enter the war against Germany?

3. What made the Ludendorff Offensive different from previous attacks on the Western Front?

4. Why did the Austro-Hungarian empire cease to exist at the end of 1918?

5. When and how did the First World War come to an end?

Unit 1: The First World War
Votes for women

At the beginning of the twentieth century, women throughout the world were still treated as second-class citizens and were not allowed to vote. This would begin to change.

The growth of factories in the nineteenth century had meant that the range of jobs available to women broadened. In the UK by 1911, there were 600 000 women working in the textile industry alone. Other women worked as domestic maids and cooks, shop assistants or secretaries. Even while women's employment broadened, however, the majority still worked either in their own homes or in industries traditionally considered 'women's work' such as the production of clothes.

Despite these limited moves towards women's independence, many people's attitudes towards women's rights remained the same. It was still widely believed that men and women occupied naturally different roles in life: men could be leaders, intellectuals and full-time wage-earners, while women belonged in the home doing the necessary work to support their husbands or fathers. Women were viewed almost like children: they were thought to have simpler minds and to be less capable of grasping complex issues. To many, the suggestion that women should be allowed to vote in elections seemed nonsensical and even dangerous.

A WOMAN'S MIND MAGNIFIED

Anti-suffrage posters attempted to make a mockery of women

Campaigns for women's suffrage

Women's **suffrage**, meaning the right to vote, became a prominent issue in the late nineteenth century, as women in multiple countries began to campaign for equal political rights with men. In 1893, New Zealand – a self-governing colony within the British Empire – became the first country in the world to give women the right to vote. In 1902, Australia became the first nation to allow women both to vote and to stand for Parliament. In the UK by this time, some women had the right to vote in local elections. But national suffrage was the real goal.

There were two very different movements for women's suffrage in the UK. The more moderate activists were called the **Suffragists**. Led by a woman named Millicent Fawcett, the Suffragists believed in winning the right to vote through logical argument and direct negotiation with politicians. Their key argument was that as Parliament made laws that women were required to obey, then women should have a say in making those laws. Men's typical counterargument was that women had (or should have) husbands or fathers who voted on their behalf and in their interests, and so they did not need the vote themselves. The main Suffragist organisation was the National Union of Women's Suffrage Societies (NUWSS), which was founded by Millicent Fawcett and had a membership of over 100 000 by 1914.

Property rights

The right to vote was not the only fundamental right that early feminists had to fight for. In 1882, married British women won the right to own their own property, which previously had automatically transferred to their husbands. When Millicent Fawcett's purse was stolen, the thief was charged by the police with 'stealing from the person of Millicent Fawcett a purse containing £1 18s 6d, the property of Henry Fawcett'.

Other women, however, believed that men would not consent to share power unless they were pushed into reform by more direct means. The **Suffragettes** were women who fought for the vote through public marches and protests, and later through violence against property. This movement was based in the Women's Social and Political Union (WSPU), founded in 1903 by Emmeline Pankhurst and her daughters. Pankhurst held meetings and rallies across the country, and the Suffragettes became known for their bold, uncompromising demands for women's independence. Beginning in 1909, the Suffragettes also attacked the property of opponents of women's suffrage – smashing windows, bombing mailboxes, and bombing and setting fire to empty buildings.

More than a thousand women were arrested for participating in the Suffragettes' campaigns. In prison, many of them went on **hunger strike** in order to call attention to their cause. In order to stop these women from dying, which would have made them martyrs and won immense public sympathy, prison wardens brutally force-fed them. Another response, licensed by a 1913 law called the Prisoners (Temporary Discharge for Ill-Health) Act (dubbed the 'Cat and Mouse Act'), was to release hunger strikers until their physical condition improved, and then re-arrest them. Nonetheless, the Suffragettes did gain a martyr in 1913 when Emily Davison was killed by the King's horse at a popular horse race called the Epsom Derby. It seems she was trying to attach a Suffragette banner to the galloping horse, but she was trampled and killed.

A suffragette protest in London

Wartime and victory

During the First World War, when many of the country's young men were fighting at the front, women's labour suddenly became vastly more important. Women threw themselves into war work and made a vital contribution to the war effort, winning a great deal of public support in the process – even though many jobs did not last beyond the war. In 1918, Parliament passed the **Representation of the People Act**, giving the right to vote to all women over thirty who were married, local government voters, or owned property. In the same year, the Parliament (Qualification of Women) Act allowed women to stand as candidates for Parliament. The first woman to take her seat as an MP, Nancy Astor, was elected in 1919. Finally in 1928, the **Equal Franchise Act** gave all British women equal voting rights with men.

Women's suffrage campaigns in some parts of Europe were not completed until much later, with French women gaining the vote only in 1945, and Swiss women in 1971. By the middle of the century, however, women's right to vote was accepted throughout most of the Western world.

Check your understanding

1. How did women's employment change in Britain during the nineteenth century?
2. What were the main differences in approach between the Suffragists and the Suffragettes?
3. What did imprisoned Suffragettes do in order to call attention to their struggle?
4. What impact did their role in the First World War have on women's campaigns for suffrage?
5. When did British women finally gain equal voting rights with men?

Unit 1: The First World War
Knowledge organiser

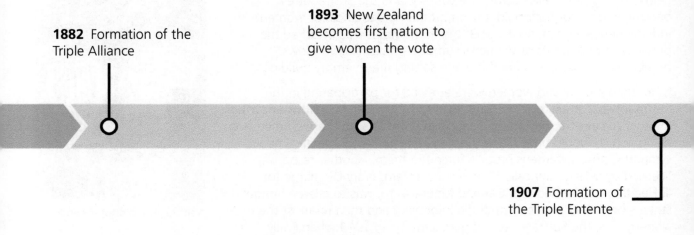

1882 Formation of the Triple Alliance

1893 New Zealand becomes first nation to give women the vote

1907 Formation of the Triple Entente

Key vocabulary

Armistice Agreement to stop fighting

Artillery Heavy, wheeled guns that fire large explosive shells

Austria-Hungary Central European empire that disintegrated after the First World War

Balance of power Situation in which peace is preserved because opposing nations have roughly equal power

Balkans South-eastern region of Europe with a complex mixture of national and ethnic groups

Black Hand Serbian nationalist terrorist organisation

Blockade Use of warships or other military force to stop a nation from trading by preventing ships from delivering and collecting supplies

Equal Franchise Act Law that gave British women full equal voting rights with men

Great War Alternative name for the First World War

Hundred Days Offensive Allied offensive that ended the war in 1918

Hunger strike Refusal by prisoners to eat any food, as a form of protest

Isolationism National policy of avoiding becoming involved in other nations' problems or conflicts

Lusitania (RMS) British passenger ship (carrying some American passengers) sunk by a German U-boat in 1915 with the loss of 1198 lives

No Man's Land Term for the area between two opposed trench systems (not held by either side)

Representation of the People Act Law that gave British women partial voting rights and the Parliament (Eligibility of Women) Act 1918 allowed them to stand for Parliament

Schlieffen Plan German plan to avoid fighting France and Russia at the same time by attacking France first and later Russia

Somme (Battle of the) Long and destructive battle fought in 1916 by the British on the Western Front along the River Somme

Suffrage The right to vote

Suffragettes Women's suffrage campaigners who believed in using direct action and civil disobedience

Suffragists Women's suffrage campaigners who believed in debate and negotiation

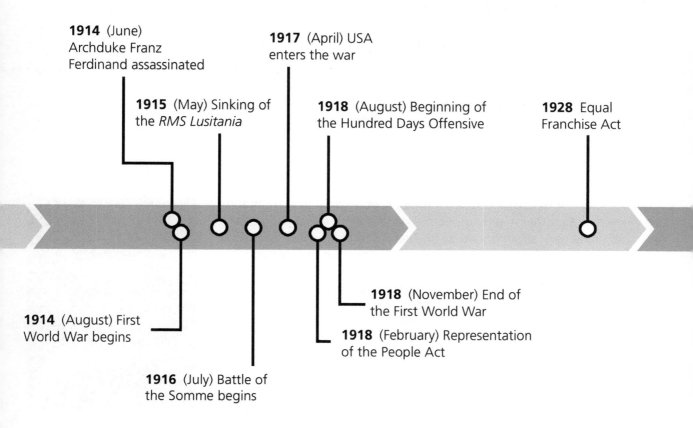

1914 (June) Archduke Franz Ferdinand assassinated

1917 (April) USA enters the war

1915 (May) Sinking of the *RMS Lusitania*

1918 (August) Beginning of the Hundred Days Offensive

1928 Equal Franchise Act

1914 (August) First World War begins

1918 (November) End of the First World War

1918 (February) Representation of the People Act

1916 (July) Battle of the Somme begins

Trench warfare Warfare based in defensive trench systems, in which neither side can gain the advantage

Triple Alliance Defensive pact formed in 1882 between Germany, Italy and Austria-Hungary that bound them to support each other in the event of war

Triple Entente Defensive alliance formed in 1907 between Britain, France and Russia ('entente' means 'agreement' in French)

U-boat German term for a submarine

Verdun (Battle of) German assault on the French in 1916 named after a small city in Northern France

War of attrition Warfare focused on forcing the enemy to use up their men and resources until they can no longer fight

Western Front Area of battle during the First World War in Belgium and France, consisting of Allied and German trench systems facing each other

Key people

Otto von Bismarck Politician who created a united Germany and became its first chancellor

Millicent Fawcett Main leader of the Suffragists and founder of the NUWSS

Archduke Franz Ferdinand Heir to the throne of Austria-Hungary, whose assassination sparked the First World War

Douglas Haig British general who launched the Battle of the Somme

Erich von Ludendorff German general who commanded Germany's war effort towards the end of the war

Emmeline Pankhurst Main founder of the WSPU, commonly known as the Suffragettes

Gavrilo Princip Serbian assassin from the 'Black Hand' who shot Franz Ferdinand

Kaiser Wilhelm II Emperor of Germany before and during the First World War

Woodrow Wilson American president from 1913 to 1921 who brought the USA into the war

Unit 2: Rise of the dictators
Marx and Russia

In October 1917, a group took power in Russia who based their politics on the ideas of the German philosopher and economist Karl Marx.

The development of Marxism

Marx was born in Germany, but spent the bulk of his adult life in London. He worked as a journalist and author, but was never financially successful and spent long periods supported by his friend Friedrich Engels, the son of a wealthy factory owner. Marx believed that industrial **capitalism** inevitably led to widening inequality, as the mass of working people (whom he called the **proletariat**) lived in squalor and deprivation, while the rich few amassed huge profits. He predicted that capitalism must inevitably collapse, as the proletarians would sooner or later rise up to seize control of the system for themselves. The workers would then create a new society based on the equal distribution of land, food and resources. This was the theory of **communism**.

Karl Marx (1818–1883)

Russia in the early twentieth century was the last place that anyone expected a communist revolution to occur. Under its **Tsars**, Russia was a mostly unmodernised country in which a small number of nobles dominated a large population of peasants. The Tsar held absolute power, industry and commerce lagged behind the other powers of Europe, and there was no political freedom. In Marxist thinking (see box), Russia had not yet even undergone its bourgeois revolution, so was nowhere near ready for a proletarian revolution.

Marxist theory

Marx's beliefs were first set out in a short book called the **Communist Manifesto**, which he co-authored with Engels. The *Communist Manifesto* was published in 1848, at a time when uprisings were fuelling fear of revolution across Europe, something alluded to in the book's opening line: 'A spectre is haunting Europe – the spectre of communism.'

In the decades that followed, Marx expanded his theory in a much longer book called **Das Kapital**. He argued that the transformation of society goes through stages. First there is a bourgeois revolution, as the middle class dismantles the Feudal System, removes the old aristocracy and creates a capitalist society. This, he argued, had already happened in most of Europe, with the upheavals of the Industrial Revolution and the French Revolution. Next would come the uprising of the proletarians, who would overthrow the capitalist **bourgeoisie** and build a communist, or socialist future (the term 'socialist' has a variety of meanings, but is often used as a synonym for 'communist').

The February Revolution

Among the Russian people, there was widespread discontent and resentment towards the Tsarist system. The desire for change was intensified by the hardships of the First World War, which took the lives of an estimated 1.8 million Russian men on the Eastern Front, and created chronic shortages of food and fuel. In February 1917, a women's demonstration in Petrograd (now called St Petersburg) sparked a series of strikes and demonstrations that brought 200 000 protesters onto the streets. The uprising quickly spread to peasant revolts in the countryside, protests in other major cities, and soldiers' and sailors' mutinies. The Tsarist system collapsed almost overnight, and the Tsar was taken prisoner by the revolutionaries.

There was immediate disagreement over what should replace the Tsarist system. A collection of officials from the Tsar's government formed a **Provisional Government** to run the country until something new could be established. Real control, however, lay elsewhere. During the February Revolution, striking workers and soldiers across the country had formed independent governing councils to make collective decisions and oversee reforms. These councils were called '**Soviets**'. It was the Soviets, and above all the Petrograd Soviet, that exercised practical control over the country and could influence or direct the workers and soldiers.

The Russian people were calling for a democratic parliament, redistribution of land, stable food supplies and, above all, an end to the war. As the year dragged on, the Provisional Government proved unable or unwilling to introduce any of these changes, and frustration grew. 'All power to the Soviets!' became the rallying cry of the revolution. There were mass desertions from the front as soldiers, unwilling to continue fighting a war they viewed as meaningless, left the trenches. Angry and desperate for change, many Russians threw their support behind the one political party who seemed willing to take direct action: the **Bolsheviks**.

The October Revolution

At this point, most Russian Marxists, including the leaders of the Petrograd Soviet, still believed that Russia was not socially developed enough for a proletarian revolution. The Bolsheviks thought differently. They were a radical faction of Russian Marxists led by a passionate and determined man named Vladimir Lenin.

Vladimir Lenin (1870–1924)

Lenin believed that a disciplined group of revolutionaries could seize power on behalf of the workers, even if the workers themselves were not yet 'ready' for power. This is just what the Bolsheviks did in the October Revolution, Russia's second revolution of 1917. Supported by a rapidly growing movement of workers and soldiers, the Bolsheviks overthrew the Provisional Government and established a dictatorship claiming to represent the workers – the 'dictatorship of the proletariat'. The world's first communist state was born.

Check your understanding

1. What did Karl Marx predict would eventually happen to capitalist society?
2. Why did Marxists consider Russia an unlikely location for a communist revolution?
3. Why did a revolution occur in Russia in February 1917?
4. Why was there mass dissatisfaction with the Provisional Government in the months following the February Revolution?
5. Why did the Bolsheviks seize power in Russia in October 1917?

Unit 2: Rise of the dictators
The USSR

The Bolsheviks transformed Russia into the **Union of Soviet Socialist Republics (USSR)**, or Soviet Union. Far from liberating the workers, however, the USSR evolved into a brutal dictatorship.

The Russian Civil War

Opposition to the Bolshevik seizure of power erupted immediately. From 1918 to 1922, Russia was involved in a civil war, as anti-Bolshevik forces called 'the Whites' attempted to reverse the October Revolution. Britain, France, America and multiple other nations all sent troops to fight alongside the Whites. The Western governments were worried about communist revolution and sought to suppress the Bolsheviks before their example could spread to other nations. The Whites were mostly led by former Tsarist officers, and they massacred peasants and performed mass public torture in order to establish their dominance. The Bolsheviks were just as ruthless, killing tens of thousands of rebel soldiers and peasants who refused to obey their directives.

The Russian Revolution, civil war and drought led to famine in Russia

As many as eight million Russians died in the civil war, around four times the Russian death toll in the First World War. During the conflict, the Bolsheviks instituted conscription, confiscated food supplies to feed their **Red Army**, and imprisoned and murdered political opponents in the 'Red Terror'. The Red Army won because it was disciplined, united and had strong leadership in Leon Trotsky. The peasants generally supported the Bolsheviks because they feared a return of the landlords if the Whites won, even though the war effort caused many of them to lose faith in their new leaders.

The struggle for leadership

In January 1924, Lenin died following a stroke. For the next four years, senior members of the Communist Party competed with each other to determine who would succeed him as leader. One of these competitors was the General Secretary of the Party, Josef Stalin (a name he chose himself, meaning 'Man of Steel'). Though he had never previously attracted much attention, Stalin was ambitious. By 1928, he had outmanoeuvred his main rival for the leadership, Trotsky. The widely admired Red Army commander was exiled from the USSR, and all power was now concentrated in the hands of Stalin.

Josef Stalin (1878–1953)

Stalin's Russia

Under the dictatorship of Stalin, the USSR became a **totalitarian** state. Though the Communist Party claimed to rule on behalf of the people, there was no democracy. Any opposition to Stalin's policies was labelled 'bourgeois' or 'counter-revolutionary', and thus declared illegal. Alternative ideologies were suppressed, including religion; the Orthodox Church was banned and driven underground. For ordinary people, the only way to improve their impoverished living conditions was to join the Communist bureaucracy that directed and supervised the work, housing arrangements and personal affairs of every citizen. If they were loyal to the Party, met their targets as workers or managers and obeyed every instruction, they hoped to be safe from persecution.

Stalin knew that Russia lagged behind the West in economic development. He therefore launched a series of Five-Year Plans: ambitious programmes of industrialisation, building factories and driving up production at speed in order to strengthen and modernise the Soviet empire. In effect, Stalin was directing an attempt to reproduce the Industrial Revolution on a dramatically compressed timescale. The project was a success in industrial terms, but at the cost of extensive human suffering as Russian labourers were literally worked to death. It also led to vast food shortages, including a famine in the Ukraine in 1932–33 that claimed 4.5 million lives.

Paranoia and terror

The regime was paranoid, like Stalin himself. In the USSR, there was no law in the conventional sense. Instead, anybody suspected of dissent, even of having disloyal thoughts, could be imprisoned, tortured or executed. The NKVD (Stalin's secret police) had spies and informers far and wide. The slightest remark hinting at dissatisfaction with the regime could lead to a swift arrest. This led to people denouncing others to get rid of people they disliked, so Stalinism spread mistrust through Russian society.

In the Great Terror of 1936–38, Stalin's suspicion of internal opponents escalated to extreme heights. High-ranking figures from the upper reaches of the Party were put on trial in public show trials – staged performances in which, after extensive torture behind the scenes, they were forced to confess to crimes before being shot. An estimated 93 out of 139 members of the Party's Central Committee were arrested, as Stalin purged anyone who might threaten his control. In total, seven to eight million people were arrested in the Terror, and 1–1.5 million were shot. In addition, between seven and eight million people now lived in the USSR's vast network of prison camps, where death rates from forced labour were high. The dream that many had of communist liberation had turned into a nightmare.

Trotsky in exile

As Stalin's rule grew increasingly cruel, the exiled Trotsky became a figurehead for all who imagined an alternative, better form of communism. Eventually, Stalin decided that it was too dangerous to let him live and sent assassins to find and kill him. In 1940, a Spanish-born NKVD agent tracked Trotsky down in Mexico and murdered him with an ice pick.

Leon Trotsky (1879–1940)

Check your understanding

1. Why did Western governments aid the Whites in the Russian Civil War?
2. What methods did the Bolsheviks employ in order to win the Russian Civil War?
3. Who were the main candidates for leadership of the Soviet Union after Lenin's death?
4. What was the purpose of Stalin's Five-Year Plans?
5. How did Stalin's paranoia grow worse during the last years of the 1930s?

The rise of Hitler

The end of the First World War brought no true peace to Germany. Instead, the country entered a period of chaos that eventually led to a whole new terror for Europe.

The Treaty of Versailles

At the Paris Peace Conference of 1919, the victorious Allies produced the **Treaty of Versailles**, which dictated the terms of the peace to the Germans. This treaty provoked anger in Germany and was seen as a national humiliation. Many on the Allied side correctly predicted that the perceived harshness of the treaty would fuel German resentment, increasing the risk of future conflict. The French general Ferdinand Foch stated: 'This is not a peace. It is an armistice for twenty years.'

Weimar Germany

The German imperial government was replaced by a democracy known as the **Weimar Republic**, named after the city where its constitution was designed. The republic was never fully accepted by many German people, in part because of its association with the humiliation of Versailles. The loss of Germany's status as a great power, and the chronic economic turmoil suffered after the war, were both blamed on the democratic Weimar government. The desperate state that Germany was in following the war gave rise to new, more extreme political views.

One of these extremists was a young **anti-Semitic** nationalist named Adolf Hitler. In 1921, Hitler became the leader of a small far-right group called the National Socialist German Workers' Party (NSDAP), popularly dubbed the **Nazis**. Hitler inspired intense loyalty in those following him. He was a talented **demagogue**, attracting crowds of supporters through his intensely emotional speeches. He gathered a small but devoted following, dedicated to the overthrow of the Weimar government and the creation of a new German empire that would be racially 'pure' and militarily expansionist.

Hitler was inspired by the **fascist** movement in Italy, led by Benito Mussolini. Mussolini seized power in 1922 and turned Italy into the world's first fascist state. Hitler wanted the same for Germany. In November 1923, in Munich, Hitler attempted to seize power. This has become known as the Munich or **'Beer Hall' Putsch** as the Nazis seized control of three leading politicians who were meeting in a large Beer Hall called the 'Bürgerbräukeller'. The putsch was a failure, the leading Nazis were arrested, and Hitler was sentenced to five years in prison. However, he only served nine months due to political pressure from his supporters. Hitler used his time in prison to write a biography and manifesto that summarised his core beliefs: ***Mein Kampf*** ('My Struggle').

Terms of the Treaty of Versailles

Under the terms of the treaty, Germany was required to:
- give up 13 per cent of its territory
- reduce its army to a mere 100 000 men
- give up its air force
- pay war reparations of 132 billion gold marks (£6.6 billion)
- formally accept responsibility for causing the war.

The signing of the Treaty of Versailles

Adolf Hitler (1889–1945)

Economic collapse and the rise of Nazism

For the next five years, the Nazis existed on the fringes of German politics, never gaining more than three per cent of the vote in national elections. The economic turmoil of the early 1920s had settled down into peace and prosperity, and few Germans paid attention to Hitler. But in 1929, economic disaster struck. The **Great Depression**, a worldwide financial collapse that began in the USA, crippled the German economy. Unemployment soon reached six million (over a third of the workforce), while wages dropped to less than two thirds of their former level and production was almost halved. Millions of shops and businesses closed down, and the state was unable to provide money, jobs, or even food for most of the unemployed. Desperate and struggling to survive, many Germans were pushed towards extreme solutions.

Hitler now found that a wider audience was ready to listen to him. He blamed all of Germany's problems, from the current economic disaster to the humiliations of Versailles and even the defeat in the First World War, on groups he identified as unpatriotic domestic enemies: democrats, socialists and, above all, Jews. Support for the German Communists was also growing, and many Germans felt that Hitler was the only politician tough enough to prevent a communist takeover.

The original publication of *Mein Kampf*

Hoping that Hitler could restore German power, the German people began to seriously listen to the Nazis. The party's electoral support peaked at 37 per cent in the election of July 1932, making them the largest party in the Reichstag (German parliament). However, they still didn't have enough seats to form a government.

Hitler comes to power

On 30 January 1933, President Hindenburg reluctantly appointed Hitler as the new Chancellor (the head of the German government). This was part of a deal whereby the Nazis would join with Germany's traditional right-wing parties to form a coalition government. Hindenburg and his allies were conservatives who hoped to restore the pre-First World War authoritarian system. They believed that, by bringing Hitler into their government, they could harness his popular support to advance their own agenda. But by making him Chancellor, they handed him the power to destroy not only them, but the entire existing order in Germany.

What is fascism?

Fascism is a political ideology of the extreme right. At its core is an aggressive and intolerant nationalism, which glorifies the nation and its leader above all else. This nationalism almost always has a strong racist component: often defined in terms of a specific ethnic group, with other ethnic groups having no true place in the nation.

Check your understanding

1. Why was the Treaty of Versailles seen as a humiliation by many Germans?

2. How was Hitler inspired by Italian politics?

3. What were the consequences of Hitler's first attempt to seize power?

4. How did the Great Depression facilitate the rise of the Nazis?

5. Why did Hindenburg appoint Hitler as Chancellor in January 1933?

Unit 2: Rise of the dictators
Nazi Germany

Once in power, Hitler eliminated all domestic opposition,
transformed Germany into a fascist state and began the
persecution of German Jews.

The Nazi takeover

Within six months of being appointed Chancellor, Hitler had moved all
political power into the hands of the Nazis. In January 1933, all political
parties apart from the Nazis were banned, and government institutions
throughout Germany converted themselves into Nazi institutions rather
than be dissolved. Following a mysterious arson attack on the Reichstag
building, Hitler passed emergency decrees that allowed him to bypass
parliament and grant extreme powers to the police. Political opponents
were arrested and imprisoned in their tens of thousands. When
Hindenburg died in 1934, Hitler combined the roles of President and
Chancellor, becoming known as the **Führer** - a German term that means
'Leader'. His new German empire was called the **Third Reich**.

A Hitler Youth poster: 'Youth serves
the leader'

The Nazis engineered popular support through the masterful use of
propaganda. They appealed to the idea of a racial 'people's community'
that could sweep away all divisions between classes and political
parties, uniting all ethnic Germans in the spirit of national pride
and national renewal. After years of division and desperation, many
Germans responded with great emotion to the Nazis' call for strength
through unity, and to their radical rejection of the past. All of these ideas
were embodied in the person of Hitler, who was presented to the German
people in almost mystical terms as a kind of national saviour.

Many Germans experienced the 1930s as very good years, infused with
a sense of optimism, excitement and even a spirit of adventure. Life was
drastically different, however, for those who were deemed to lie outside
the bounds of the 'people's community'.

Jews in the Third Reich

At the heart of Nazi ideology was a vicious anti-Semitism.
Jewish people had lived in Germany for over a thousand
years, but Hitler regarded them as a corruption within
the national community. He believed that white Germans
represented the ideal racial type, which he called the
'**Aryan race**'. German Jews never made up more than 1
per cent of the population and were well integrated into
German society, but Hitler claimed that they threatened
the very existence of Germany, poisoning German culture
from within, and controlling both communism and
international high finance.

Windows of a Jewish-owned shop smashed during
Kristallnacht

These views were not unique to Hitler or even to Germany. Extreme anti-Semitism was common in Europe in the first half of the twentieth century, and so the Nazis' message of hate fell on fertile ground.

In the Third Reich, German Jews experienced a gradual escalation of anti-Semitic measures over many years, as their persecution was slowly normalised.

In 1933, Jews were excluded from the civil service as government jobs were reserved for ethnic Germans. Soon afterwards, the Nazis began systematically forcing them out of their homes and businesses, driving many to leave Germany altogether. Then, in September 1935, came the **Nuremberg Laws**, two laws that effectively created a segregated society.

The SS and violent persecution

Nazi anti-Semitism was overseen and enforced by an organisation called the **SS** (*Schutzstaffel*), meaning the 'Protection squad'. Originally Hitler's private bodyguards, the SS had grown into an army of elite, ideologically driven Nazi troops. Under their commander, Heinrich Himmler, the SS ran the Nazi surveillance network, the security and criminal police, and a network of **concentration camps** for political prisoners. They were instrumental in the persecution of German Jews that intensified during the 1930s.

This persecution took it's most violent form yet in the massive **pogrom** on the night of 9 November 1938. Nazi mobs attacked Jewish property, burned synagogues, and killed and wounded hundreds of Jewish people. Because of the smashed windows of Jewish homes and shops, this pogrom became known as ***Kristallnacht*** – the 'Night of broken glass'.

The killing of the disabled

In 1939, the Nazis began committing their first organised, systematic murders. The victims were the physically or mentally disabled, who were regarded as a burden on society and a corruption of the German race. The Nazis described these people as 'life unworthy of life'. Parents of disabled children were encouraged to admit their children to special treatment wards, where they would be secretly killed. The so-called euthanasia programme was soon extended to adult mental asylum patients who were deemed unfit to live. They were killed in gas vans: converted vans that enabled poisonous carbon monoxide exhaust fumes to be pumped into a sealed inner chamber. This organised killing foreshadowed the infamous programme of systematic murder that was soon to follow: the genocide of the European Jews.

The Nuremberg Laws

- The Reich Citizenship Law declared that only ethnic Germans qualified for citizenship. Jews were instead classed as state subjects with no citizenship rights.
- The Law for the Protection of German Blood and German Honour forbade marriage and sexual relations between Germans and Jews.

Non-Jewish victims

Though Jews held a central place in the Nazi ideology of prejudice, they were not the only group to be persecuted. Roma (gypsies), Jehovah's Witnesses, black people, the mentally ill, the disabled, LGBT people, alcoholics, the homeless, repeat criminals and the unemployed all faced similar discriminatory measures.

Check your understanding

1. What made the Nazi government appealing to many Germans?
2. How did Hitler view the Jewish people of Germany?
3. What were the provisions of the Nuremberg Laws?
4. What role did the SS play in Nazi Germany?
5. What was the Nazi policy towards the physically and mentally disabled?

Unit 2: Rise of the dictators
The road to war

Once Hitler came to power, he worked to prepare Germany for the next war: a war he would launch in order to establish Germany's supremacy in Europe.

Hitler planned to expand German territory by wars of conquest in order to create *Lebensraum* ('living space') for the German people, principally in eastern Europe. He began a massive rearmament programme, manufacturing weapons, planes and other military equipment. This broke the terms of the Treaty of Versailles, but brought Germany back to full employment, aiding a remarkable economic recovery.

In 1936, Hitler stationed troops in the vital industrial region known as the **Rhineland**, which had been made a demilitarised zone by the Treaty of Versailles. The French and the British chose not to oppose this move, deciding that opposing Hitler's attempts to restore German strength could cause another European war. This policy became known as **appeasement**. In Germany, meanwhile, the remilitarisation of the Rhineland was widely seen as a triumph as it rebelled against the hated Treaty of Versailles.

The Spanish Civil War

By the end of 1936, the Nazis had negotiated alliances with fascist Italy and Japan, creating what became known as the **Axis**. Very soon afterwards, both Germany and Italy took an opportunity to test the power of their rapidly growing armies. From 1936 to 1939, a bloody civil war was fought in Spain. On one side were the Republicans – an alliance of democrats, socialists, trade unionists and other left-wing groups. Opposing them were the supporters of an attempted military takeover led by General Francisco Franco. Franco was backed by the traditional powers in Spanish society: wealthy landowners, the army and the Catholic Church. To many observers, the Spanish Civil War was symbolic of the broader struggle between fascism and democracy taking place across Europe.

The British and French, again seeking to avoid conflict, did not send military aid to the Spanish Republicans. By contrast, Hitler and Mussolini enthusiastically sent troops to fight for Franco. An elite German military unit called the Condor Legion effectively used the Spanish Civil War as a training ground for newly developed military tactics, including strategic aerial bombing. With the help of fascists from across the continent, Franco won the war and became Europe's newest dictator. Hitler's soldiers returned home, tested in battle and ready to be deployed against other enemies.

Francisco Franco (1892–1975)

The Third Reich expands

In 1938, Hitler embarked on an ambitious programme of territorial **annexations** around the borders of Germany. Its neighbour Austria was German-speaking and largely enthusiastic for unification, so was peacefully absorbed into the Third Reich by an act of union called the *Anschluss*. Hitler's next target was Czechoslovakia, which he now began making plans to invade. In a series of meetings with Hitler in September 1938, the British Prime Minister Neville Chamberlain convinced him instead to annex only the Sudetenland, a German-speaking border region of Czechoslovakia. Additionally, Chamberlain made Hitler promise that this would be his final territorial acquisition in Europe. This settlement, which was made without consulting the Czech people, was known as the **Munich Agreement**. Chamberlain, a firm believer in appeasement, confidently declared that with this deal he had secured 'peace for our time'. These illusions were shattered in March the next year when Hitler annexed most of the remainder of Czechoslovakia.

Neville Chamberlain on a visit to Munich in 1938

Hitler's next move astonished the international community. Hatred of communism was almost as fundamental to Hitler's worldview as hatred of Jews, and throughout his career, he had condemned the Bolsheviks as deadly enemies of Germany. Hitler had repeatedly declared that the Third Reich and the Soviet Union must sooner or later come to conflict. Yet on 23 August 1939, Hitler and Stalin shocked the world by signing the **Nazi–Soviet Non-Aggression Pact**, which bound them not to attack each other.

Hitler still intended to invade the USSR eventually, but he wished to avoid fighting a two-front war in both west and east simultaneously, as Germany had done in the First World War. He therefore planned to turn on Russia only when he had neutralised other threats. Until that day, the Nazi–Soviet Pact bought him time and left him free to initiate other wars of conquest in Europe without the fear of Soviet interference.

The invasion of Poland

One week after the pact was signed, on 1 September 1939, Hitler invaded Poland. This moment marked the beginning of the Second World War, and two days later, the British and French declared war on Germany. It was too late to save Poland, which was soon invaded a second time: from the east, by the Soviet Union. Stalin was taking advantage of his alliance with Hitler to seize the eastern half of the country for the USSR. The conquest of Poland took little more than a month, as the two dictators divided the country between them. The British and French Allies, meanwhile, prepared to meet Hitler's next attack.

Check your understanding

1. How did Hitler secure the loyalty of the German army?
2. Why was it such a triumph for Hitler to station troops in the Rhineland in 1936?
3. What allowed Franco and his followers to win the Spanish Civil War?
4. How did Hitler expand the Third Reich before the outbreak of the Second World War?
5. Why was the Nazi–Soviet Pact met with astonishment in Europe?

Unit 2: Rise of the dictators
Knowledge organiser

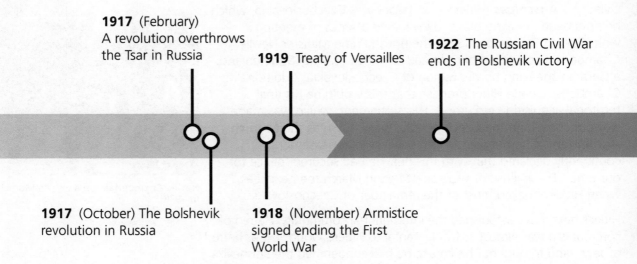

1917 (February)
A revolution overthrows
the Tsar in Russia

1919 Treaty of Versailles

1922 The Russian Civil War
ends in Bolshevik victory

1917 (October) The Bolshevik
revolution in Russia

1918 (November) Armistice
signed ending the First
World War

Key vocabulary

Annex Take over a territory, usually by force

Anschluss Peaceful annexation of Austria by the Third Reich

Anti-Semitism Prejudice and hatred of Jewish people

Appeasement British and French policy of allowing Hitler to take what he wanted in the hope that this would avoid war

Aryan race An idealistic race that the Nazis believed white Germans represented

Axis Alliance between Nazi Germany, fascist Italy, and Japan

'Beer Hall' Putsch A violent uprising in the city of Munich in 1923; it was the first attempt by Hitler to seize power

Bolsheviks Radical Russian Communist party who founded the USSR

Bourgeoisie The middle class, or those who make money through trade or industry

Capitalism Social system based on the freedom to buy, sell and trade

Communism Social system based on the equal distribution of land and resources

Communist Manifesto Short book by Karl Marx and Friedrich Engels that lays out the basic ideas of Communism

Concentration camp A guarded compound where people are held prisoner in harsh conditions with no rights

Das Kapital Book by Karl Marx explaining his theories in detail

Demagogue Politician who wins support by appealing emotionally to people's desires and prejudices

Fascism Political ideology based on nationalism, racism and intolerance of opposing ideas

Führer German term meaning 'Leader', used to refer to Hitler

Great Depression Severe worldwide economic collapse that lasted for much of the 1930s

Kristallnacht Massive pogrom against German Jewish communities and property in 1938

Mein Kampf Book written by Hitler outlining his beliefs

Munich Agreement Treaty that briefly prevented Hitler from invading Czechoslovakia

Nazis Anti-Semitic fascist German party, led by Adolf Hitler

Nazi–Soviet Non-Aggression Pact Agreement between the Third Reich and the USSR, stating that they would not attack each other

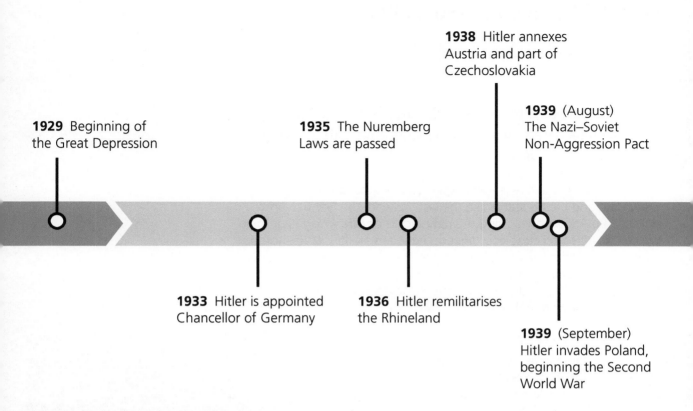

1929 Beginning of the Great Depression

1933 Hitler is appointed Chancellor of Germany

1935 The Nuremberg Laws are passed

1936 Hitler remilitarises the Rhineland

1938 Hitler annexes Austria and part of Czechoslovakia

1939 (August) The Nazi–Soviet Non-Aggression Pact

1939 (September) Hitler invades Poland, beginning the Second World War

Nuremberg Laws Laws that stripped German Jews of citizenship and forbade them from marrying or having sexual relations with non-Jewish Germans

Pogrom Violent attack on a minority group, usually Jews

Proletariat The working class, or those who depend on wage labour for their living

Provisional Government Temporary government formed to govern Russia after the February Revolution

Red Army The army of the USSR

Rhineland Major industrial region of Germany

Soviet Originally a council of workers or soldiers formed in Russia after the February Revolution; later a term for citizens of the Soviet Union

SS (*Schutzstaffel*) The military unit that carried out Nazi policies

Third Reich Germany under the Nazis, expressing desire to build a new German empire

Totalitarianism Any political system that aims for total control over all aspects of people's lives

Treaty of Versailles Treaty that formally ended the First World War and penalised Germany

Tsar Emperor of Russia before the revolution

Weimar Republic Democratic government of Germany between the abdication of Kaiser Wilhelm II and the Nazi takeover

USSR Communist regime in Russia, also called the Soviet Union

Key people

Neville Chamberlain British Prime Minister who supported appeasement and convinced Hitler to sign the Munich Agreement

Francisco Franco Fascist dictator of Spain

Adolf Hitler Leader of the Nazi party and fascist dictator of Germany

Vladimir Lenin Leader of the Bolsheviks, who launched the 1917 October Revolution and created the USSR

Karl Marx German economist who developed the theory of Communism

Benito Mussolini Fascist dictator of Italy

Josef Stalin Dictator of the USSR, who seized power after Lenin's death

Leon Trotsky Stalin's main rival for leadership of the USSR

Unit 3: The Second World War
The war in Europe

In a series of rapid and devastating campaigns, the Nazi war machine took barely two years to bring almost all of Europe under Axis domination.

Most of Europe's military leaders expected this second war to be long drawn out and mostly static, like the last. Instead, the German army pulled off quick victories using the new tactics of **_Blitzkrieg_** ('lightning war'). This relied on close coordination between artillery, truck-borne infantry and fighter planes, all moving at speed and mounting sudden, concentrated attacks. In the spring of 1940, Hitler seized Denmark, Norway, the Netherlands, Belgium and northern France. Greece and Yugoslavia followed in the spring of 1941.

The fall of France

Of all these campaigns, the most dramatic and shocking to the Allies was the conquest of France, which took less than six weeks in May and June 1940. The German army effectively sliced the Allied army in two, trapping 400 000 Allied soldiers in a small pocket of north-eastern France and Belgium. As the Germans closed in, nearly 340 000 of these men were desperately evacuated to Britain through the port of **Dunkirk**. If the Royal Navy's rescue operation had not been successful, Britain's capacity to continue fighting would have been severely limited.

The evacuation of thousands of allied troops from Dunkirk

France was forced to surrender to Germany. Under the terms of surrender, around three-fifths of France, including its entire Atlantic and North Sea coast, was occupied by the Reich. The remainder of the country was allowed to remain theoretically independent under a conservative government based at **Vichy**, which actively cooperated with the Nazis for the rest of the war. In western Europe, this left the UK facing Germany alone.

The Battle of Britain

Germany now focused on conquering Britain, but before any invasion could be launched, they needed to subdue the **Royal Air Force (RAF)** and secure supremacy in the skies. Between July and October 1940, the **Battle of Britain** was fought in the skies above southern England – the area of Britain closest to the German-controlled airfields on the continent. When the battle began, the **Luftwaffe** (German air force) had over 1000 fighter planes and almost as many bombers. The British had around 900 fighter planes, most of them either the iconic Spitfire or the less famous but more effective Hurricane.

North Africa

In June 1940, Italian forces based in Libya (an Italian colony) attacked British Egypt, with the goal of seizing the Suez Canal. For the next three years, the British and the Axis engaged in a struggle for control of the North African coastline, which ended only with the expulsion of all Axis forces from Africa in May 1943.

The defence of Britain was successful, due in part to the recent invention of **radar**. A network of radar stations precisely detected the numbers, position and direction of incoming German planes, while real-time communication with RAF fighters in the air allowed them to intercept the enemy squadrons. By mid-autumn, British pilots and radar operators had ensured that British airspace would remain under British control. In the House of Commons, Prime Minister Winston Churchill declared: 'Never in the field of human conflict was so much owed by so many to so few.'

The Nazi–Soviet war

With his control of continental Europe secure, Hitler felt free to turn his attention to the Soviet Union. On 22 June 1941, Hitler broke the Nazi–Soviet pact by marching three million German troops into the USSR in **Operation Barbarossa** – the largest invasion in human history. The Soviet Union joined the war on the Allied side, and the British (and later the Americans) found themselves in an uneasy alliance with the communist dictator Stalin.

From its outset, the Nazi–Soviet war was characterised by destruction on an unprecedented scale. German soldiers were indoctrinated to view the people of eastern Europe as racially inferior and to fear the Soviet Union as the source of a Jewish conspiracy to undermine German civilisation. They therefore indiscriminately burned towns, massacred civilians and exploited prisoners for slave labour.

At first the Germans won multiple victories, while the Soviet armies retreated in disarray. But the *Blitzkrieg*'s reliance on rapid, constant movement and regular attacks proved impossible to sustain in the vast spaces of Russia. Not only that, Hitler had gambled on securing victory before winter, and so most of his troops were not supplied with winter clothing. As temperatures plummeted, rain dissolved the fields into mud, thick snow blocked the roads, and countless soldiers succumbed to frostbite. The German advance slowed and slowed.

In the first week of December, fighting in temperatures of –30°C, a German army failed to capture Moscow and was forced to a halt less than 50 kilometres from the city. With the failure to seize the capital, the momentum of the German invasion was lost. The Nazi–Soviet war shifted into an attritional struggle. The odds were stacked against Germany, which did not have the manpower reserves or the industrial capacity to continue pouring armies into the east. Over the coming years, the effort to sustain the conflict with Russia would strain Germany to breaking point.

Wartime propaganda poster featuring Stalin

The Soviet death toll

Over seventy million people died in the Second World War. Around half of these were from the Soviet Union, including civilians. Accurate figures are very difficult to determine, but it seems that more than ten million Soviet civilians were killed in German massacres or died of famine and disease when their homes were destroyed.

Check your understanding

1. How did the Germans achieve such rapid and decisive victories?

2. Why was the evacuation from Dunkirk so critical for Britain's war effort?

3. How were the British able to win the Battle of Britain?

4. In what ways did the Russian campaign present unique challenges to the German armies?

5. Why was the failure to achieve victory in Russia before winter such a disaster for the Germans?

Unit 3: The Second World War
The British home front

The Second World War led to profound changes in British society, even as it imposed great hardship and privations for the vast majority of civilians.

Churchill as Prime Minister

The failure of appeasement left Neville Chamberlain's reputation in ruins. On 10 May 1940, the same day as the invasion of France, Winston Churchill replaced him as Prime Minister at the head of a coalition. Churchill was 65 years old and his career up to this point had been marked by controversy. He was a committed supporter of British imperialism, staunchly opposed Indian independence and was widely seen as a war-monger. Much of the nation, including the royal family, backed Churchill's rival for the post – Lord Halifax, the Foreign Secretary. Churchill derived moral authority, however, from the fact that he had opposed appeasement and spent much of the 1930s warning of the threat posed by Hitler.

In the event, Churchill's energy, assurance and steadfast determination made him a successful wartime leader. Where Halifax had suggested negotiating a peace, Churchill pledged 'to ride out the storm of war, and to outlive the menace of tyranny, if necessary for years, if necessary alone'.

Winston Churchill (1874–1965)

Churchill's speeches

Churchill inspired the nation by the power of his rhetoric, and his speeches were instrumental in maintaining British morale. In a famous speech, given after the evacuation from Dunkirk, Churchill declared: 'We shall fight on the beaches, we shall fight on the landing grounds, we shall fight in the fields and in the streets, we shall fight in the hills; we shall never surrender.'

The Blitz

Since the Battle of Britain began, the Luftwaffe had been bombing British airfields in order to destroy the RAF's repair and refuelling stations. Midway through September 1940, however, they switched to bombing cities. This was the bombing campaign known as the **Blitz** (not to be confused with *Blitzkrieg*). The Blitz brought terror to British civilians. In a campaign lasting until May the next year, the Luftwaffe launched 71 major bombing raids on London and dozens more on other major cities, including Coventry, Bristol, Birmingham, Glasgow and Liverpool. However, the Blitz did bring relief to the RAF and thus proved to be a tactical error by Hitler.

A German bomber flying over London

The objective of the Blitz was to blockade Britain by destroying shipping and ports. On the first day alone, after the bombing of London's docklands, a fire spread that is estimated to have caused more damage than the Great Fire of 1666.

People in cities grew used to the sound of air-raid sirens, and every night a blackout was imposed in order not to present visible targets to the bombers above. People hid and slept in cellars, bomb shelters and in the London underground. When the Blitz ended, there was some respite, but late in the war the Germans developed new means of attack: V-1 flying bombs and so-called V-2 rockets, both of which were pilotless missiles fired at Britain from launch sites in France, Belgium and the Netherlands. In all, just over 60 000 British civilians died in bombing throughout the war and many more lost their homes.

Total war

Wartime Britain was governed by a policy known as **total war**. This meant in effect that the whole of society was mobilised for warfare, chiefly through a massive expansion of British industry in order to produce the necessary quantities of war material. Over half the population came to be employed by the government. The state imposed steep tax hikes, longer working hours and strict rationing for all staple foods (except potatoes and bread).

There was near-universal consensus that the war was both necessary and just, and so the British remained united behind the war effort. Nonetheless, it came to be widely felt that the sacrifices demanded by total war ought to be honoured by the state after the war. In November 1942, the economist William Beveridge released a report outlining a welfare system to combat what he called the five great evils in modern society: squalor, ignorance, want, idleness and disease. The report proposed that all working people should pay regular national insurance (a new form of tax) in order to fund unemployment support, pensions and other social benefits. It also called for the provision of universal healthcare.

The **Beveridge Report** gave substance to the notion that Britain was fighting not just to defeat Nazism, but for the opportunity to build a better nation after the war. In the election of July 1945, a month after Germany was defeated, the British rejected Churchill for Clement Attlee's Labour government. This government would use the Beveridge Report as the basis for building the postwar welfare state.

Evacuation

In order to protect them during the Blitz, over a million children were evacuated from London and other cities to spend the war living in homes in the countryside. Many were billeted with complete strangers.

Tube stations in London doubled as air raid shelters

Women's economic emancipation

The British workforce grew by over half a million during the war, and around 80 per cent of these new workers were women. Eight times as many women did government work in the Second World War as in the First, and they were drawn from all social classes and walks of life. Several key industries were principally staffed by women, including Britain's munitions factories and its all-important rail network. Women were paid less than men and often struggled with the combination of long working hours and continuing domestic duties.

Check your understanding

1. Why was Churchill in some respects an unlikely choice of Prime Minister?
2. What was the impact of German bombing on British civilians?
3. How did daily life change due to the demands of total war?
4. How did the war increase women's participation in the workforce?
5. What were the recommendations of the Beveridge Report?

The Holocaust

Between 1941 and 1945, the Nazis attempted to murder all European Jews. This genocide has come to be known as the **Holocaust.** Jewish people call it the Shoah.

The killing of Jews on the Eastern Front

From the beginning of his dictatorship, Hitler believed that the German community needed to be 'purified' by the elimination of what he regarded as Jewish racial poison. However, by 1941 the German Reich had spread through Poland and into Russia, two countries with far larger Jewish populations than Germany. For this reason, Hitler formed four SS killing squads, known as **Einsatzgruppen**, to accompany the German armies into Russia and to slaughter all the Jews they found. These men would ultimately kill around 1.3 million Jews, mostly by firing squad. It was expected that the remaining Jews in the Soviet Union would die from starvation and overwork under Nazi occupation.

The killing in the course of Operation Barbarossa was the beginning of the Nazi genocide. However, Hitler and the SS wanted a more systematic approach to exterminating Jewish people, so devised a new plan to intensify their programme. Known as the 'Final Solution', this was the plan to establish a network of death camps in occupied Poland. At a conference at **Wannsee** (a suburb of Berlin) on 20 January 1942, senior Nazi officials agreed to the mass deportation of Jews to the east. The conference set the number to be killed at eleven million. In the end, the Nazis would kill six million.

The death camps

Soon after Wannsee, a programme of mass deportations to the new killing centres began. In all Nazi-occupied parts of Europe, Jews were rounded up by the **Gestapo** (Nazi police) or by collaborating local police. They were told they were being resettled in new communities in the east and were packed onto trains. During a journey that could take as long as eleven days, they were given very little food or water and were constantly exposed to the elements. Many died before they even reached the camps.

Of the six death camps, four existed only for murder: Treblinka, Belzec, Chelmno and Sobibor. At these camps, the vast majority of Jews would be killed in the gas chambers within a few hours of arrival. The other two, **Auschwitz** and Majdanek, were also slave labour camps. At Auschwitz, when the Jewish people arrived, they would be lined up on the platform at the railway station. An SS officer would walk down the line and select those who were fit for work, purely by glancing at them. The rest would go straight to their deaths.

Life in Auschwitz

The slogan above the iron gates of Auschwitz read, Arbeit macht frei ('Work sets you free'). In fact, the work done by inmates was designed eventually to kill them. In the vast labour camps attached to Auschwitz, Jews died from starvation, punishment beatings, exhaustion, torture, disease or medical experimentation. Almost none survived more than a year.

The main gate of the concentration camp Auschwitz, Poland

At the gas chambers, the victims were told that they were going to be given a shower. All would strip naked, and their possessions were taken away. Then the Jews were ushered into large rooms with the word 'Shower' on the doors in all major European languages and with fake showerheads on the ceilings. Once all were inside, the doors were locked. Through vents in the ceiling, a deadly gas was released (carbon monoxide at most camps, though Auschwitz used a cyanide-based gas called Zyklon B). The gas took between fifteen and thirty minutes to kill everyone inside. It would have been a very painful death.

Units of Jewish prisoners called *Sonderkommandos* ('special units') would then remove the bodies from the gas chambers and take them to the giant crematoria to be burnt. The killing process was timetabled and designed for maximum efficiency. The *Sonderkommandos* even removed hair and gold teeth from victims so that these could be sent to be used in German factories.

Late in the war, when it became clear that the Nazis were going to lose, deportations to the death camps were increased in a desperate attempt to kill as many Jews as possible. Almost half a million Jews from Nazi-allied Hungary were sent to the camps in 1944 alone. Then, as the Soviet armies approached, Jewish prisoners were marched westwards through the snow in massive death marches designed to kill them through exhaustion or exposure. Very few remained to be liberated when the Soviet army finally reached the camps.

The banality of evil

In the history of the Holocaust, it is easy to find examples of extraordinary and obvious inhumanity. However, the vast majority of Germans who participated were not sadists or psychopaths, but average, law-abiding citizens, who took these jobs because they were convenient and who did not question or criticise what they were doing. Most Germans might not have actively supported the genocide, but they did not feel strongly enough to take a stand against it. In the words of the Italian chemist Primo Levi, one of the few who survived Auschwitz: 'Monsters exist, but they are too few in number to be truly dangerous. More dangerous are the common men, the functionaries ready to believe and to act without asking questions.' The Jewish intellectual Hannah Arendt would call this phenomenon '**the banality of evil**'.

The Soviet army liberated the prisoners at Auschwitz in January 1945

Check your understanding

1. Why did Hitler send the *Einsatzgruppen* to accompany his invasion of the Soviet Union?

2. What was decided at the Wannsee conference?

3. How were Jewish people persuaded to be transported to the death camps?

4. Why did so few Jewish prisoners remain in the camps when the Soviet armies reached them?

5. How did Primo Levi and Hannah Arendt interpret the psychology of the German people who participated in the Holocaust?

The war in Asia

Simultaneously with the war in Europe, a separate conflict was fought in East Asia and the Pacific. Here the aggressor was not Germany, but Japan.

Japanese conquests in China

Japan at this time was dominated by its armed forces. One of the leading generals, Hideki Tojo, also held the post of Prime Minister in order to control the government. Military policy was focused on nationalist expansion in east Asia, beginning in China. In the 1930s, China was a fragmented nation where multiple political parties struggled for power. The most prominent was a group called the **Guomindang (GMD)**, known as the Nationalists and led by Chiang Kai-Shek, but even they were corrupt, insecure, and not strong enough to resist Japanese aggression. In 1931, Japan annexed **Manchuria** (north-eastern China), setting up a **puppet state** called Manchukuo in order to govern it. After several more years of pressure, Japan invaded China in July 1937, this time with the objective of total conquest.

Within six months, the Nationalists had been forced to abandon the northern and coastal provinces following Japanese victory in the Battle of Shanghai. They fled west into the less developed Chinese interior, and attempted to carry on fighting from the new capital of Chongqing. Effectively cut off from the outside world and with little hope of recovering territory, by 1941 the Nationalists were on the verge of defeat.

> ### The 'Rape of Nanjing'
>
> In December 1937, Japanese forces seized the city of Nanjing, the GMD capital just upriver from Shanghai. There followed a deliberate outbreak of mass rape and murder by Japanese soldiers that left an estimated 200 000 to 300 000 dead.

Pearl Harbor

The Japanese generals and admirals next planned a campaign of conquest to bring huge swathes of south-east Asia under their rule. The objective was to secure control of the region's resources and especially its oil. The one great obstacle to this plan was the USA, which alone possessed the military might to oppose Japan in the Pacific. Before attacking its Asian neighbours, therefore, Admiral Isoroku Yamamoto, who was chief of the navy, insisted that Japan carry out a pre-emptive strike the USA's naval base at **Pearl Harbor** in Hawaii.

This was the principal base of the American Pacific fleet. An attack on Pearl Harbor could destroy so many ships as to render the USA incapable of serious naval operations. In the early morning of 7 December 1941, a force of 183 Japanese warplanes attacked the base, catching the Americans by surprise. A second wave of 170 warplanes attacked an hour and a half later. Dozens of ships and almost 200 aircraft were damaged or destroyed by the bombing.

The battleship *USS Arizona* sinking after being hit by Japanese air attack

The US President Franklin D. Roosevelt had supported the Allies since the beginning of the war. However, he could not formally end American neutrality because of the strength of isolationist feeling among American voters. The attack on Pearl Harbor changed this. With near-unanimous political support, Roosevelt declared war on Japan and on its ally, Germany. The American economy was reorganised for war; by 1943, American factories were producing the same number of aircraft as had been destroyed at Pearl Harbor every two days. The quantity of armaments that the USA could produce was enough to sustain the Allied war effort. Germany and Japan struggled to secure enough resources and maintain enough factories to match American production.

Winston Churchill, Franklin D. Roosevelt and Josef Stalin at the Yalta Conference, 1945

The Pacific war

After Pearl Harbor, Japan's wave of conquests continued according to plan. In the first six months of 1942, the Japanese brought one-sixth of the surface of the planet under their rule, easily capturing Hong Kong, Burma (now Myanmar), Malaya, the Philippines, most of the Dutch East Indies (now Indonesia), and the western Pacific islands. The British colony at Singapore (a Royal Navy base regarded as one of the great fortresses of the empire) fell on 15 February when 140 000 soldiers and civilians were captured.

The new Japanese empire was officially called the 'Greater East Asian Co-Prosperity Sphere', as the Japanese claimed to be liberating Asian people from their colonial masters. In reality, Japanese rule was often far more severe than European rule. Over ten million civilians in China alone, and millions more in south-east Asia, were forced into labour in which hundreds of thousands died. Around 400 000 women, mostly Korean and Chinese, were forced to become sex slaves for Japanese soldiers. They were euphemistically known as 'comfort women'.

Japanese expansion was halted at the naval **Battle of Midway** in June 1942, when American forces destroyed enough Japanese aircraft carriers and planes as to make further conquests unfeasible. The Americans then began the process of reconquering the Pacific from Japan, one island at a time. The USA also supplied and aided Chiang's Nationalists, whose continued resistance kept around a million Japanese troops in China rather than fighting the Americans. Over years of bitter warfare, the frontiers of the Japanese empire were slowly pushed back.

Check your understanding

1. How did Japan take advantage of China's weakness during the 1930s?
2. Why did Japan attack Pearl Harbor on 7 December 1941?
3. How did the attack on Pearl Harbor bring the USA into the war?
4. Why were Allied prisoners of war treated so brutally by their Japanese captors?
5. How did the USA halt the expansion of the Japanese empire in June 1942?

Japanese war crimes

Japanese treatment of prisoners of war was notoriously inhumane. This was partly due to a military code of honour that regarded surrender in any circumstances as shameful: in the eyes of many Japanese, Allied soldiers who had allowed themselves to be captured alive were dishonoured and unfit to live. Prisoners were routinely tortured, executed or worked to death, often while building railways and other infrastructure in the conquered territories. This was all in violation of internationally agreed codes of conduct for the treatment of prisoners of war.

The end of the war

By 1943, it was clear that Germany had reached the limits of its expansion and was on the defensive. Yet it would take another two and a half years before the Axis powers finally surrendered.

A second German offensive in the Soviet Union had culminated in a brutal five-month battle in the city of **Stalingrad**. When the German attackers surrendered in February 1943, the Nazis were forced to begin the long retreat from Russia. Soviet armies spent the next two years pushing them back to Germany.

The Battle of Stalingrad

The bombing of Germany

While the Soviets were advancing, the British sought to wear down the Germans through an airborne bombing campaign. Air Chief Marshal Arthur 'Bomber' Harris developed the controversial strategy of **area bombing** or carpet bombing, destroying large urban areas, including some entire cities, in order to crush the morale of the civilian population. Around 400 000 German civilians were killed, and almost five million left homeless, by Allied bombing. The most damaging attacks used incendiary bombs to create massive firestorms that could reach 1600°C. Historic German cities, including Hamburg and Dresden, were destroyed in this way.

The defeat of Germany

On 6 June 1944, code-named **D-Day**, a massive Allied invasion force landed on the beaches of Normandy. This was the product of over two years of secret and obsessively detailed planning by Churchill, Roosevelt and their generals. The man chosen to direct the invasion was the American Dwight D. Eisenhower, who was appointed supreme commander of the Allied Expeditionary Force in Europe.

The strategy for **Operation Overlord** relied on the use of overwhelming force to punch through the German coastal fortifications. Shortly after midnight on 6 June, thousands of parachutists were dropped into Normandy, tasked with destroying bridges and railways in order to prevent German reinforcements from reaching the coastline.

Breaking Enigma

German military communications were encrypted using an ingenious coding machine called **Enigma**. Breaking the Enigma codes would allow the Allies to track and anticipate the movements of German U-boats, thus protecting the trans-Atlantic supply lines on which the war effort depended. The Enigma codes were deciphered by a team led by the brilliant mathematician Alan Turing, working at **Bletchley Park**, the British code-breaking centre. After the war, Turing's electro-mechanical code-breaking machines became the foundation of computer science.

As dawn broke a fleet of 5000 ships began landing soldiers and tanks on five beaches (code-named Utah, Omaha, Gold, Juno and Sword) spread over an 80-kilometre section of the Cotentin peninsula. In a hail of machine gun fire, men got out of their landing craft, often into deep water, and fought their way ashore through barbed wire and anti-personnel mines. Once on the beaches, they had to assault the concrete fortifications that the Germans had constructed to defend France's Atlantic coastline. It took the entire day, with the landings supported by intensive naval bombardment. By nightfall, all five beaches had been captured by the Allies.

From this foothold, the Allied armies could begin battling their way across Europe, liberating France before advancing into Germany. As the Red Army closed in from the east, Germany was squeezed between enemies on both frontiers. Vast areas of the country were physically wrecked, while hundreds of thousands of German soldiers died in a series of final, futile attempts to defend their homeland. On 30 April 1945, in a bunker beneath Berlin, Hitler committed suicide by shooting himself in the head. One week later, on 8 May, Germany surrendered unconditionally to the Allies.

American troops going ashore on D-Day

The defeat of Japan

In June 1945, the island of Okinawa, the last Japanese stronghold in the Pacific outside Japan itself, fell to the Americans after three months of fighting. The battle of Okinawa cost the lives of 108 000 Japanese and 12 000 American troops. By this point, a six-month campaign of aerial firebombing had destroyed dozens of Japanese cities. Japan retained control of parts of China and south-east Asia, but their defeat was now clear.

Stalin had promised that he would declare war on Japan three months after the defeat of Germany. He was true to his word: in the early hours of 9 August, the USSR launched an invasion of Japanese-occupied Manchuria, Korea and Sakhalin. However, by this time, the USA had already delivered its own knockout blows.

The aftermath of the Hiroshima atom bomb

The atomic bomb, the most destructive weapon ever invented, was developed during the last years of the war in an American research programme called the **Manhattan Project**. In July 1945, the world's first nuclear bomb was detonated in the New Mexico desert. On 6 August, the USA dropped a nuclear bomb on the Japanese city of Hiroshima. Three days later, a second bomb was dropped on Nagasaki. To this day, these remain the only nuclear weapons ever to have been used in war. Several weeks later, on 2 September 1945, Japan surrendered.

Check your understanding

1. What was the purpose of Arthur Harris' area-bombing campaign?
2. Why was it so vital for the Allies to break the Enigma codes?
3. What made the D-Day landings so challenging and so dangerous for the Allied armies?
4. How had the USA established dominance in the Pacific by mid-1945?
5. What new weapons did the USA use against Japan in August 1945?

The destroyer of worlds

The physicist heading the Manhattan Project, J. Robert Oppenheimer, said that when he witnessed the first nuclear explosion he recalled a line from the ancient Hindu text, the *Bhagavad Gita*: 'Now I am become Death, the destroyer of worlds.'

Unit 3: The Second World War
Knowledge organiser

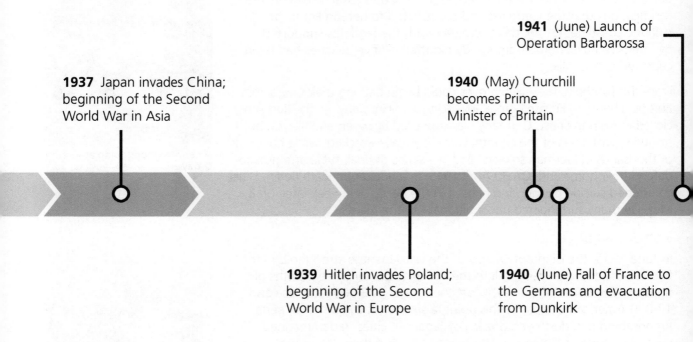

1937 Japan invades China; beginning of the Second World War in Asia

1941 (June) Launch of Operation Barbarossa

1940 (May) Churchill becomes Prime Minister of Britain

1939 Hitler invades Poland; beginning of the Second World War in Europe

1940 (June) Fall of France to the Germans and evacuation from Dunkirk

Key vocabulary

Area bombing Also called carpet bombing, the strategy of bombing a large civilian area instead of specific military targets

Auschwitz Largest of the six Nazi death camps

Banality of evil The idea that ordinary people can commit war crimes if they are willing to uncritically follow orders

Battle of Britain German attempt in 1940 to gain control of British airspace in order to prepare for an invasion

Beveridge Report Wartime report by William Beveridge on poverty and inequality in Britain

Bletchley Park The British code-breaking centre

Blitz Bombing of Britain by the Germans

Blitzkrieg 'Lightning war'; German term for warfare using fast-moving, mechanised units supported by fighter planes

D-Day Allied invasion of Nazi-occupied France

Dunkirk French port from which Allied troops were evacuated to Britain after the fall of France

Einsatzgruppen SS death squads that accompanied Operation Barbarossa in order to kill Jews

Enigma German coding machine used to encrypt military communications

Gestapo Nazi police, who rounded up Jews to deport them to the death camps

Guomindang (GMD) Chinese party known as the Nationalists who governed China before and during the Second World War

Holocaust Genocide of the European Jews by the Nazis

Luftwaffe The German air force

Manchuria North-eastern China

Manhattan Project American research project that developed the first nuclear bomb

Midway (Battle of) Naval battle at which the USA inflicted enough damage on the Japanese fleet to prevent further conquests (a turning point in the Pacific war)

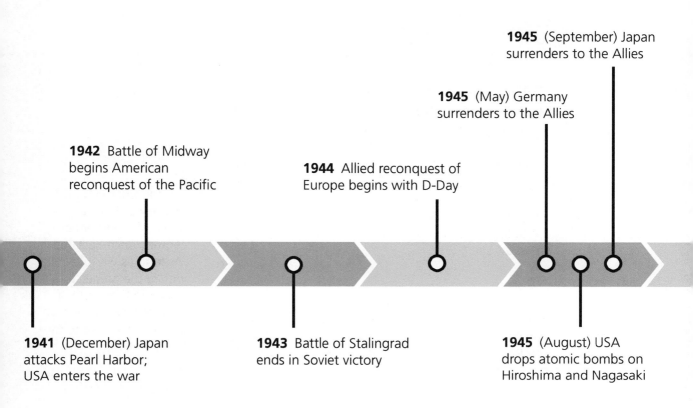

1942 Battle of Midway begins American reconquest of the Pacific

1944 Allied reconquest of Europe begins with D-Day

1945 (May) Germany surrenders to the Allies

1945 (September) Japan surrenders to the Allies

1941 (December) Japan attacks Pearl Harbor; USA enters the war

1943 Battle of Stalingrad ends in Soviet victory

1945 (August) USA drops atomic bombs on Hiroshima and Nagasaki

Operation Barbarossa Hitler's invasion of the USSR in 1941

Operation Overlord Code name for the Allied invasion of Normandy in June 1944

Pearl Harbor American naval base in Hawaii, headquarters of the Pacific fleet

Puppet state A state that is theoretically independent, but in practice controlled (like a puppet) by another country

Radar Technology that locates and tracks objects by bouncing radio waves off them

RAF Royal Air Force, the British air force

Stalingrad (Battle of) Massive battle in the USSR (1942–1943) that forced the Germans to begin retreating

Total war Policy of mobilising an entire society and economy for a war effort

Vichy France Area of France under the pro-Nazi government that collaborated with Hitler

Wannsee Conference Conference in January 1942 at which senior Nazis agreed to the deportation of Jews to be killed in Poland

Key people

Hannah Arendt Jewish historian and philosopher who developed the concept of the 'banality of evil'

Clement Attlee British Prime Minister who replaced Churchill in 1945

Winston Churchill Wartime Prime Minister of Britain

Dwight D. Eisenhower American general who commanded the Allied armies in Europe from D-Day until the end of the war, later a president of the USA

Arthur Harris Head of Britain's Bomber Command

Chiang Kai-Shek GMD leader who commanded China before and during the war

Franklin D. Roosevelt President of the USA during the war

Alan Turing British mathematician who led the team that broke the Enigma codes and seen as a founder of computer science

Unit 4: Decolonisation
Decolonising India

After the Second World War, the European colonial empires began to collapse. The largest of these empires was the British, whose two-century-long rule of India was coming to an end.

Six years of warfare had left the French, Dutch, Italians and British severely weakened. Rebuilding their own countries would be hard, but hanging on to their overseas colonies would prove impossible. Independence movements were pushing for power all across Asia and Africa. It soon became clear that the Second World War had brought the age of European imperialism to an end.

Indian nationalism

Indian tax revenue provided the British Empire with a vital income, while Indian troops were key to its defence. In the First World War, no fewer than 1.3 million Indian soldiers and labourers fought and worked for the British Empire. But the **Raj** was already being undermined from within by a steadily growing nationalist movement.

This movement was based in the Indian National Congress (often called the **Congress Party**), a predominantly Hindu political group founded in 1885. Though it still pledged 'unswerving loyalty' to the British crown, the British authorities viewed the Congress Party as a threat and refused to cooperate with it.

During the First World War, Prime Minister David Lloyd George drew up plans to introduce complete self-government for India gradually, while keeping it within the Empire. In 1919, however, the British administration in India not only failed to honour these promises of self-government, but passed a law called the Rowlatt Act that allowed Indian activists to be arrested and imprisoned indefinitely without trial. Riots broke out in response. At Amritsar, on 13 April, Colonel Reginald Dyer ordered his troops to fire on a crowd of unarmed protesters. Over 400 Indians were killed. The **Amritsar massacre** remains one of the most notorious atrocities in the history of British colonial rule.

After Amritsar, Indian nationalism became focused and radicalised, as many Indians concluded that the British would only give up control of India when forced to. The man who now emerged as leader of the independence movement was a Hindu lawyer and activist named Mohandas Gandhi. He was known by the honorary title Mahatma, meaning 'Great Soul'. Gandhi led a campaign of **civil disobedience**, which included strikes, boycotts of British courts and schools, refusal to serve in British government jobs, refusal to pay taxes, sitting and blocking streets, and hunger strikes in prison. Gandhi's non-violent strategy became an inspiration to independence movements across the world. For many Indians, he came to be viewed almost as a holy man.

Indian rule

George Curzon, British **viceroy** of India at the dawn of the twentieth century, once declared: 'As long as we rule India, we are the greatest power in the world. If we lose it, we shall drop straightaway to a third-rate power.'

Divide and rule?

Many Indians suspected the British of pursuing a 'divide and rule' strategy, controlling India by discouraging Hindus and Muslims from uniting against them. The most controversial example was Lord Curzon's proposal in 1905 to **partition** the province of Bengal, dividing it into a Hindu-majority province and a Muslim-majority province. The British claimed the purpose was to protect the Muslim minority from a repressive Hindu majority, but their policies often had the effect of fuelling tension and resentment between India's two main religious communities.

Gandhi's leadership and prestige also helped to hold the nationalist movement together, smoothing over divisions between Hindu and Muslim activists. Despite this, by 1930, Muslim nationalists were arguing that when independence was won, there should be a separate nation for Muslims created in India's north-west.

When Japanese armies advanced across Asia in 1942, the Congress Party called upon Britain for immediate independence by passing the '**Quit India**' resolution. In response, the British arrested tens of thousands of Congress leaders, including Gandhi, and banned the party. Protests erupted across India, and over 100 000 people were imprisoned. The British ruled India under martial law for the remainder of the war. In the process, they oversaw a devastating famine in Bengal in 1943, in which around three million Indians died. Many Indians blamed the famine on British occupation policy, which involved printing money to pay for wartime costs and thus driving up prices uncontrollably.

Mahatma Gandhi (1869–1948)

Indian independence

When Clement Attlee's government came to power in 1945, it offered full independence to India and declared that it would hand over control no later than June 1948. This extremely short timetable prompted both Hindu and Muslim nationalists to push for the partition of India into separate nations, having no time to negotiate a compromise that might have held them together. As a result, on 15 August 1947, two new nations came into being: India and Pakistan.

Immediately there were massive population transfers, as Hindus and Muslims migrated between the two countries to ensure they lived under a government of their own religion. In areas where minorities were left stranded, tens of thousands of people were massacred. Gandhi was assassinated in January 1948 by a Hindu extremist for attempting to halt the violence.

People migrating to their chosen nation during the Indian partition

Check your understanding

1. How was it believed the British were using a 'divide and rule' strategy to govern India?

2. What was the Amritsar massacre?

3. How did Mahatma Gandhi use civil disobedience to campaign for Indian independence?

4. How did Britain respond to the 'Quit India' resolution in 1942?

5. Why did the creation of India and Pakistan lead to violence in both nations?

Unit 4: Decolonisation
Decolonising the Middle East

British imperial rule in the Middle East was a much more recent phenomenon than in India, and yet it would leave an even more complex and troubled legacy behind it.

Until the early twentieth century, most of the Middle East was ruled by the **Ottoman Empire**. For centuries this formidable Turkish power had ruled over the Arab people of the region. In 1914, however, the Ottomans joined the First World War on the side of the Central Powers. This would prove to be their downfall.

Britain and the Arabs

Britain, which had ruled Egypt informally since 1882, now declared an official protectorate and proceeded to use Egypt as its base for launching attacks on the Ottoman Empire. The British hoped to bring down the empire from within by supporting the Arab tribes who were already pushing for independence. In 1916, the British recognised Hussein bin Ali, Sharif (ruler) of Mecca, as independent ruler of the Hejaz (western Arabia). In June that year, Hussein began the **Arab Revolt**, a rebellion against Ottoman rule that was armed and supported by the British.

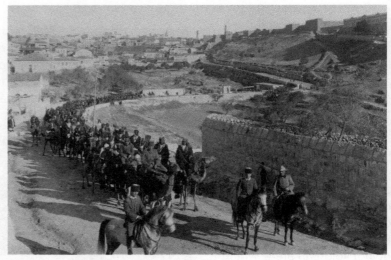
The Arab army during the Arab Revolt

Hussein was promised the rule of the entire Ottoman Middle East. Secretly, however, the British had already made plans to keep the Ottoman territories for themselves. In May 1916, the diplomats Sir Mark Sykes of Britain and François Georges-Picot of France made a secret agreement to divide the Middle East between their two empires, with France to get what became Syria, and Britain to get what became Iraq and Jordan. The Arab inhabitants of the region were not consulted.

In 1918, following successes by the combined Arabic and British armies, the Ottoman Empire collapsed. It would be replaced in its heartland by the modern nation-state of Turkey, founded in 1923. All its territories beyond Turkey fell to the imperial powers of Europe. The new nations of Syria, Iraq and Jordan, created on the basis of the **Sykes–Picot Agreement**, were artificial: their borders were lines drawn on a map, with no resemblance to the actual divisions between the ethnic and religious groups living there. As a result, the British and French struggled to impose unity on their new imperial possessions. They also faced insurrection in all three countries, as the Arabs, feeling betrayed, fought for their independence.

The problem of Palestine

Among the promises made by the British to Hussein and his allies was that the Arabs of Palestine, the coastal region containing Jerusalem, would have their independence. Palestine, however, was also the focus of an international movement among some sectors of the Jewish community. This was **Zionism**, the movement to establish a nation-state for Jewish people in their ancient homeland. In 1917, the British officially declared their support for Zionism in a statement known as the **Balfour Declaration**. In effect, the British had now promised the same piece of land to two different groups of people.

After the First World War, Britain took over the administration of Palestine. At this time there were around 600 000 Arabs living in Palestine and around 80 000 Jews. Jewish immigration increased, especially as the Nazis gained power in Germany and Jewish refugees fled Europe to Palestine in the hope of safety. This increase in numbers resulted in tension and there were frequent anti-Jewish riots by the Arabs. In 1937, a British government report concluded that the claims of the two sides were incompatible. By the 1940s, there was constant guerrilla warfare in Palestine between Jewish and Arab militant groups.

British withdrawal

Recognising the reality of Arab nationalism, the British granted partial independence to Jordan in 1928 and to Iraq in 1932. However, in the Second World War both grants of independence were revoked. It was vital for the Allies to protect their supply of oil from the Middle East in order to keep their planes and ships running, and so both Iraq and Jordan were reoccupied. Only after the war did the British finally withdraw fully from the region, as did the French from Syria. All three countries would face troubled futures, due in part to the artificiality of the borders and institutions forced on them by Europeans.

Because of the Holocaust and with the emergence of a strongly pro-Zionist policy in the United States, there was widespread international support after the Second World War for the creation of a Jewish state in Palestine. On 14 May 1948, the nation of Israel was officially proclaimed. It was immediately attacked by Egypt, Jordan and Iraq, expressing the outrage of much of the Arab world. Israel won this war, but the future appeared uncertain. A massive 750 000 Palestinian Arab refugees were soon living in camps in Jordan and Egypt. The displacement of these Palestinians bred a huge amount of mistrust and hatred towards the new state of Israel. Recurring violence between Arabs and Israelis has continued to the present day.

Saudi Arabia

In the Arabian peninsula to the south of Iraq, a long-running struggle for power between Hussein and a rival Arab king, Abdulaziz (called 'Ibn Saud' by Westerners), ended in victory for Abdulaziz in 1932. Abdulaziz and his family, the **House of Saud**, established the new kingdom of Saudi Arabia. The kingdom would grow immensely rich, thanks to newly discovered reserves of oil.

Check your understanding

1. How did Britain attempt to undermine the Ottoman Empire during the First World War?
2. How did the Sykes–Picot Agreement reorder the Middle East?
3. Why were there competing claims for control of Palestine from the First World War onwards?
4. Why did the British reoccupy Jordan and Iraq during the Second World War?
5. Why did many Arabs resent the creation of the state of Israel?

Unit 4: Decolonisation
Decolonising Africa

The British Empire in Africa consisted of over 20 colonies covering huge areas of the continent. By the mid-1960s, almost all were independent.

The Suez Crisis

The British had granted partial independence to Egypt in 1922, but kept control of the Suez Canal. The canal remained vital for Britain's empire because of the access it provided to India and Middle Eastern oil. However, in 1952 British control of the canal came under threat when a revolution in Egypt brought a group of anti-British army officers into power. The man who now became president of Egypt was named Gamal Abdel Nasser. He was an inspirational leader who soon came to be regarded as a global hero of anti-colonialism. A committed Egyptian nationalist, Nasser wanted the British to leave Egypt for good.

Gamal Abdel Nasser (1918–1970)

In July 1956, Nasser **nationalised** the Suez Canal, placing it under the direct control of the Egyptian government. Outrage erupted in Britain. The canal was widely seen as a vital possession in Britain's shrinking empire, and much of the public was affronted at the thought of losing it. Prime Minister Anthony Eden believed that Nasser was a new Hitler, who, if not stopped, would begin a career of destructive conquests. Eden therefore formed secret plans with France and Israel to regain control of the Suez Canal and remove Nasser from power.

In October, Israel invaded the canal zone. This was done deliberately in order to give Britain and France an excuse to intervene. Claiming that free movement through the canal was in danger, the two former imperial powers launched an airborne and seaborne invasion to 'protect' the canal. To observers worldwide, it was obvious that Britain, France and Israel had manufactured a crisis in order to take back the canal. American President Dwight D. Eisenhower (who twelve years previously had commanded the D-Day invasion) demanded that all three aggressors withdraw from Egypt. This was a shock to the British, who had assumed that the USA would support them. But Eisenhower threatened to withhold an urgently needed loan, which would have crippled the British economy. Eden was forced to call off the invasion.

Port Said after the attack of British and French troops

The Suez Crisis was a national humiliation for Britain, clearly demonstrating the loss of British status and power on the international stage. It is often seen as the definitive endpoint in the history of the British Empire as a global power.

African independence movements

Like the borders drawn up by France and Britain in the Middle East, the borders between European colonies in Africa were often little more than lines drawn on a map. Ethnic and linguistic groups were split apart and lumped together with no regard for their own identities or interests. This meant that when the European powers withdrew, the new African nations often faced futures of division, civil conflict, and the oppression or persecution of minorities.

The humiliation of the British at Suez inspired Britain's other African colonies to push more quickly for independence. The next to become independent was Ghana (formerly the Gold Coast), which gained independence in 1957. This came after almost a decade of strikes and protests led by the man who now became president, Kwame Nkrumah. He was at the forefront of a wave of independence movements driven in part by **Pan-Africanism**, which meant solidarity between all African nations and the liberation of all territories still under Western rule. After Ghana, other colonies quickly followed: Nigeria became independent in 1960, Uganda in 1962, Kenya in 1963, and Malawi and Zambia in 1964.

In the so-called settler colonies – those governed by large populations of white immigrants – independence had come much sooner. Cape Colony became a self-governing dominion under the name South Africa in 1910. Here, a white (Dutch and British) minority held power over a much larger black African majority. In 1961, they declared full independence and became a republic, largely out of fear that they would be forced to grant more rights to the oppressed black population. In 1965, Southern Rhodesia declared independence from similar motives: the white colonists hoped to retain as much control as possible over the black majority. In both South Africa and Southern Rhodesia (now called Zimbabwe), white elites had constructed deeply unjust systems of segregation, designed to keep black people in a permanently inferior position.

The Mau Mau revolt

In 1952, a group called the Land and Freedom Army, known as the **Mau Mau**, launched a violent uprising against British rule in Kenya. The British suppressed the revolt by detaining hundreds of thousands of Kenyan people in concentration camps. Prisoners in these camps died from disease, torture and forced labour. Though figures are disputed, the British are thought to have killed some 50 000 Kenyans during the revolt. A state of emergency lasted until 1960.

The Apartheid Museum in Cape Town shows an example of the segregation signs seen in the country during apartheid

The Commonwealth of Nations

Founded in 1931, the **Commonwealth** is a global association of 53 nations with strong links to the UK. Almost all of them are former colonies of the British Empire, but all share equal status within the organisation. The Commonwealth is perhaps best known today for the Commonwealth Games, a sporting competition hosted every four years by one of the Commonwealth nations.

Check your understanding

1. What was the plan devised by Anthony Eden to recover control of the Suez Canal in 1956?
2. Why was the Suez Crisis such a humiliation for Britain?
3. Why did many African nations experience serious civil conflict after gaining independence from their European colonisers?
4. How did the British suppress the Mau Mau revolt in Kenya during the 1950s?
5. Why did South Africa and Zimbabwe declare independence from Britain in 1961 and 1965?

Unit 4: Decolonisation
Irish Republicanism

In Ireland, Britain's oldest colony, the twentieth century saw a protracted struggle between those Irish who wished to remain part of the United Kingdom and those who wanted independence.

As the century dawned, Ireland was still formally part of the UK. For decades, Liberal governments had sought to introduce Home Rule for Ireland: the restoration of a parliament to Dublin, and self-government within the UK. Home Rule was the short-term goal of the Irish **Republican** movement, which represented the rural Catholic majority and ultimately aimed for full independence. However, in **Ulster** in the north of Ireland, there was a large Protestant community descended from English and Scottish settlers. These were mostly **Unionists**, meaning they wanted Ireland to remain part of the United Kingdom and be governed from London. The Unionists threatened violent uprising if Home Rule were ever introduced.

The partition of Ireland

In 1914, the British government at last passed a bill establishing Home Rule, but then delayed its implementation until the end of the war. Yet before the war could finish, one group of Republicans launched a direct attempt to wrest control from the British. On Easter Monday in 1916, around 1600 protesters led by Patrick Pearse and James Connolly took control of several public buildings in Dublin, making their headquarters in the central Post Office. They declared Ireland a republic and proclaimed themselves a provisional government. Over four days of fighting, British soldiers violently suppressed the **Easter Rising**, and its leaders were executed.

The brutality of the British response alienated huge numbers of Irish and fuelled support for full independence. In the British election of December 1918, every Irish constituency outside Ulster elected candidates from **Sinn Féin**, the leading Republican political group. Refusing to take their seats in London, the Sinn Féin candidates instead convened their own parliament in Dublin, the Dáil Éireann. In 1919, the Dáil once again declared Ireland a republic – and the Irish War of Independence erupted. Resistance to British rule was now organised by the **Irish Republican Army (IRA)**, the military wing of Sinn Féin.

The war ended in December 1921, when Michael Collins, commander of the IRA, signed the Anglo-Irish Treaty. When it came into force the next year, this made most of Ireland independent but kept six of the nine counties of Ulster within the UK. They became Northern Ireland. The new independent Irish nation immediately entered a ten-month civil war, fought between those who supported the treaty (the Free-Staters) and those Republicans who wished to continue fighting for Ulster. However, the Republicans eventually chose to accept the partition of Ireland. The island has remained divided ever since.

Lady Constance Markiewicz

One of the Sinn Féin candidates elected in 1918 was Lady Constance Markiewicz, the first woman to be elected to the UK Parliament (though she did not take her seat).

The Black and Tans

The **'Black and Tans'** (so called because of their mixture of police and army uniforms) were a group of British men recruited to reinforce the Irish police force. They were mostly former soldiers who had come straight from the Western Front and were responsible for terrible violence in Ireland, including mass rape, torture, massacres and burning down homes.

The Troubles in Northern Ireland

Northern Ireland, the newest country of the UK, was very hostile to the Catholic Irish minority in its midst. Catholics faced widespread discrimination and were shut out of key professions, including the civil service, judiciary and police. From the late 1960s to the 1990s, there was renewed violence in Northern Ireland – a period known as the '**Troubles**'.

The Troubles started when Catholic civil rights protesters in 1969 were confronted by Protestant 'loyalist' counter-protesters. The resulting violence prompted the British government to send in the army to keep the peace, but this in turn provoked further conflict. Violence between Unionist militants, Republican militants, and the British Army escalated. The most notorious incident occurred in January 1972 when British paratroopers in Derry killed thirteen civilians, an event known as **Bloody Sunday**. By the time the Troubles were over, 3600 people had been killed, and one in five Ulster residents had a family member killed or wounded in the fighting.

The key Republican paramilitary group was a new version of the Irish Republican Army, the Provisional IRA (named after the provisional government declared during the Easter Rising). This new IRA pursued a thirty-year campaign of bombings and shootings both in Ireland and on the British mainland. Their goal was to make Northern Ireland ungovernable through violence. On the opposing side, the largest Protestant militant group was the Ulster Defence Association (UDA), which, like the Provisional IRA committed frequent terrorist attacks throughout the three decades of the Troubles.

In 1997, Tony Blair's Labour government opened direct negotiations with Sinn Féin under its leader Gerry Adams. The result was the **Good Friday Agreement** of 1998, which brought an end to the Troubles. The agreement formally established the rights of the Irish nationalist minority in Northern Ireland – including guaranteed representation in a new local parliament, the Northern Ireland Assembly. It also removed border checks and instituted permanent close cooperation between the Irish and Northern Irish governments, finally restoring normal life for Irish people in both countries.

Catholic mural in Derry, Northern Ireland

Protestant mural in Belfast, Northern Ireland

Assassination attempts

The Provisional IRA made at least two attempts to assassinate a British prime minister. In 1984, Margaret Thatcher narrowly escaped being killed by a bomb in Brighton. In 1991, mortar shells were fired into 10 Downing Street while John Major was having a cabinet meeting.

Check your understanding

1. What is the difference between the Republican and Unionist movements in Ireland?
2. What were the consequences in Ireland of the British election of December 1918?
3. How did the Anglo-Irish Treaty resolve the conflict in Ireland?
4. How did the Provisional IRA attempt to end British rule in Northern Ireland?
5. Why did the Troubles come to an end in 1998?

Unit 4: Decolonisation
The wars for Vietnam

In south-east Asia, one of the most hard-fought struggles for decolonisation eventually drew in the USA. The result was a traumatic conflict that left deep scars in all nations involved.

The colonial power here was France. **Indochina**, a region encompassing the modern nations of Laos, Cambodia and Vietnam, was a major French imperial possession. French rule was swept away by Japanese conquest during the Second World War, and when Japan was defeated in 1945, the people of Indochina hoped to claim their independence. But the French wanted their colony back.

The First Indochina War

The main independent political group in Vietnam was a communist party called the **Viet Minh**, led by a veteran communist named Ho Chi Minh. During Japanese occupation, the Viet Minh had been supplied and funded by the Americans as they fought against the invaders. Yet when Ho Chi Minh declared Vietnamese independence on the day of the Japanese surrender in 1945, the Americans were reluctant to support him. With Japan and Germany defeated, the Soviet Union was already coming to be seen as the West's primary enemy. The American government wished to prevent the spread of communism anywhere in the world. They therefore supported the French attempt to regain control of Indochina.

Ho Chi Minh (1890–1969)

The First Indochina War lasted from 1946 to 1954. During this war, the Viet Minh general Vo Nguyen Giap developed a guerrilla warfare strategy that would prove almost impossible to counter. Vietnamese communist soldiers learnt to use the dense jungle to hide from the enemy, avoid open battle and instead mount surprise attacks on French army units. The French came to fear the next ambush and grew increasingly desperate as they struggled to even locate their enemy. When a large French garrison surrendered to Giap at **Dien Bien Phu** in May 1954, it signalled the end of the war. A peace agreement was signed at Geneva, and the French withdrew from Indochina.

The Vietnam War

For the Americans, this was troubling news. The USA was now deeply committed to the global confrontation with the Soviet Union that was called the Cold War (see Unit 6). The concern was that allowing the communist Viet Minh to govern Vietnam would allow communism to spread throughout south-east Asia.

The agreement at Geneva was that Vietnam would be divided temporarily, with the north to be governed by the Viet Minh and the south to become an American-allied republic. Elections to reunite the country were scheduled for 1956, but were repeatedly delayed.

Chemical warfare

American soldiers in Vietnam frequently used Agent Orange, a defoliant (chemical that makes trees shed their leaves) that also caused severe medical problems in those who were exposed to it. They also bombed villages using napalm, a highly flammable substance that clings to its targets while burning.

As the Vietnamese grew frustrated with the slow pace of change, Ho Chi Minh eventually accepted that to achieve reunification and independence he would have to fight a second war, this time against the Americans.

Communist guerrillas began attacking targets in the south in 1959, and the USA sent troops in response. American military commitments to Vietnam grew slowly through the early 1960s, with many troops officially labelled 'advisors' in order to disguise the reality that the country was entering a new war. However, in 1964 President Lyndon B. Johnson authorised a massive escalation, and it became clear that the USA was committed to the conflict. This was the Second Indochina War – more commonly known in the West as the Vietnam War.

American helicopters dropping soldiers into the jungle during the Vietnam War

Vietnamese communist soldiers, known as the **Viet Cong**, were experts in jungle guerrilla warfare. The Americans found themselves in the same position as the French, their vast military power rendered useless by an enemy they could not pin down. In addition, the Viet Cong wore no uniform, so it was impossible to tell which civilians in any Vietnamese village might in fact be enemy soldiers, waiting to strike. Fearful and paranoid, the Americans resorted to launching 'search and destroy' raids: helicopter attacks on villages that very often led to massive civilian casualties. As the war dragged on, it became increasingly clear that the USA had no hope of victory, and was achieving nothing but mass violence.

The Vietnam War was the first war to be broadcast directly into people's homes via television. This caused much of the American public, shocked by what they saw, to abandon their support for the conflict. In 1973, President Richard Nixon withdrew American troops from Vietnam. Within two years, what remained of the American-allied South Vietnamese state had been overrun, with the communists capturing the southern capital of Saigon in April 1975. Vietnam was reunited as a communist nation. In the course of the war, 58 000 American soldiers had been killed. Estimates of Vietnamese casualties range from one million to almost four million military and civilian dead. It had taken almost 35 years of fighting, against Japan, France and finally the USA, for Vietnam to gain its independence.

The massacre at My Lai

In March 1968, several hundred unarmed Vietnamese civilians were killed in their village by an American army unit on a 'search and destroy' mission. The victims were mostly women, children and old men. Many of the women were raped before their deaths. The American army attempted to cover up the **My Lai massacre**, but it was exposed by journalists and caused shame and outrage back in the USA.

Check your understanding

1. Why did the USA support the French in the First Indochina War?

2. What was the strategy developed for the Vietnamese army by Vo Nguyen Giap?

3. Why did the Viet Minh launch a second war for Vietnam in 1959?

4. What were some of the reasons why so many Vietnamese civilians were killed by the Americans during the Vietnam War?

5. How did the Vietnam War come to an end in 1975?

Unit 4: Decolonisation
Knowledge organiser

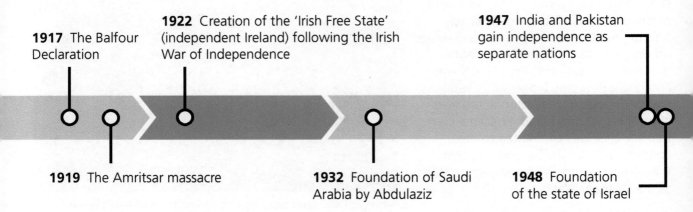

1917 The Balfour Declaration

1922 Creation of the 'Irish Free State' (independent Ireland) following the Irish War of Independence

1947 India and Pakistan gain independence as separate nations

1919 The Amritsar massacre

1932 Foundation of Saudi Arabia by Abdulaziz

1948 Foundation of the state of Israel

Key vocabulary

Amritsar massacre Atrocity in which over 400 Indian protesters were killed when British soldiers fired on the crowd

Arab Revolt Rebellion against Ottoman rule by the Arabs during the First World War, supported by Britain

Balfour Declaration British government statement establishing official support for Zionism

Black and Tans British paramilitary troops that fought in the Irish War of Independence, known for their brutality

Bloody Sunday Killing of thirteen Northern Irish civilians by British paratroopers in 1972

Civil disobedience Protest tactic based on the non-violent refusal to obey laws that are considered unjust

Commonwealth of Nations Global association of 53 nations with strong links to the UK, mostly former British colonies

Congress Party Indian National Congress, a Hindu-dominated political party that spearheaded the independence movement

Dien Bien Phu Climactic battle of the First Indochina War, resulting in a Viet Minh victory against the French

Easter Rising Rebellion against British rule in Ireland in 1916

Good Friday Agreement Agreement between the British government, Irish government, and Northern Irish parties, that ended the Troubles

House of Saud Royal family that founded Saudi Arabia and continues to govern it

Indochina Former French colony in south-east Asia that is now the nations of Cambodia, Laos and Vietnam

Irish Republican Army (IRA) Military wing of Sinn Féin, that fought for Irish independence and later (as the Provisional IRA) took part in the Troubles

Mau Mau revolt Uprising against British rule in Kenya

My Lai massacre Atrocity in which several hundred Vietnamese civilians were killed by American soldiers

Nationalise Place an industry or company under direct government control

Ottoman Empire Turkish empire that ruled the Middle East and parts of Europe and Africa from the fourteenth century to 1918

Pan-Africanism 'All-Africanism'; belief in solidarity between African nations against colonial powers, or in the unification of African nations

Partition The division of a region into two or more separate territories or nations

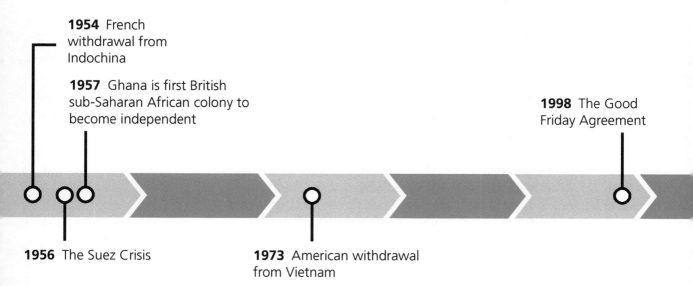

1954 French withdrawal from Indochina

1957 Ghana is first British sub-Saharan African colony to become independent

1998 The Good Friday Agreement

1956 The Suez Crisis

1973 American withdrawal from Vietnam

Quit India Resolution passed by the Congress Party in 1942 demanding the British immediately withdraw from India

Raj Term for British-ruled India from 1858 until Indian independence in 1947

Republicans In Ireland, those who supported Irish independence, later those who wished to reunite Northern Ireland with Ireland

Sinn Féin The leading Republican political party in Northern Ireland

Sykes–Picot Agreement Secret diplomatic agreement between Britain and France in 1916 to divide the Middle East between them after the defeat of the Ottoman Empire

Troubles Thirty-year period of violence between Republican and Unionist groups in Northern Ireland

Ulster The northern region of Ireland, part of which remained in the United Kingdom in 1922 and became Northern Ireland

Unionists In Ireland, those who support remaining part of the United Kingdom

Viceroy Official in charge of ruling British India

Viet Cong Term given to communist guerrillas in South Vietnam during the Vietnam War

Viet Minh Communist party and independence movement in Vietnam

Zionism The movement to establish (later to maintain) a nation state for Jewish people in the region that is now Israel

Key people

Abdulaziz Founder of Saudi Arabia, often known in the West as Ibn Saud

Michael Collins Commander of the IRA during the Irish War of Independence

Anthony Eden British prime minister during the Suez Crisis

Mohandas Gandhi Prominent leader of the Indian independence movement, who advocated non-violence and civil disobedience

Vo Nguyen Giap Vietnamese general who pioneered the tactics of jungle guerrilla warfare

Ho Chi Minh Leader of the Vietnamese communists during both Indochina Wars

Hussein bin Ali Sharif of Mecca, leader of the Arab Revolt

Gamal Abdel Nasser Nationalist president of Egypt during the Suez Crisis

The American Civil War

In the United States of America, the abolition of slavery was not achieved peacefully. Instead, the struggle grew into a massive civil war that threatened to tear the new republic apart.

When America came into being in 1776, it was already a nation divided between two societies. In the Southern states, slavery was central to American life. Around one in four families owned slaves, and plantations worked by slaves (growing cotton, sugar and tobacco) were essential to the Southern economy. In the Northern states, there were many fewer slaves, and slavery was gradually abolished during the early nineteenth century. White Southerners fought bitterly against any attempt by the Northern states to limit their rights as slave-owners.

Harriet Tubman

Harriet Tubman was a former slave who escaped and made it to the North in 1849. She then ran a series of missions into the South to rescue slaves and guide them to freedom, relying on a secret network of abolitionists and safe houses called the **Underground Railroad**. During the 1850s, Tubman successfully freed hundreds of slaves.

Harriet Tubman (1820–1913)

'A house divided'

As America expanded westward across the continent, new states were usually added in pairs, one slave-owning and one free. This meant that the divide between North and South was maintained and extended as the country grew. Southerners argued that black slaves were actually better treated than the white working class in the North and that poor white Southerners were able to live in greater dignity because the worst work was done by slaves. They also argued that black people were unable to look after themselves, and therefore that freeing them would be cruel and irresponsible.

Northerners, however, were growing increasingly uneasy with the spread of slavery and feared the growing power of Southern senators in Congress. In 1854, a new political party was founded called the **Republicans**, based entirely in the Northern states and dedicated to fighting the 'slave power'. The tension between abolitionists and slave-owners was becoming explosive.

Abraham Lincoln (1809–1865)

In the election of 1860, the Republican candidate, Abraham Lincoln, was elected president. During his campaign, Lincoln emphasised the message that America could not survive as a nation half slave-owning and half free. He famously repeated the Biblical warning: 'A house divided against itself cannot stand.' For Southerners, Lincoln's election was the final straw. Refusing to be governed by him, in December 1860, South Carolina **seceded** from the Union, officially declaring itself no longer part of the United States. The rest of the South soon followed – eleven states in total. They formed a breakaway nation, the **Confederate States of America**, with a man named Jefferson Davis as their president. Lincoln and the North were determined not to allow it. They resolved to fight to preserve the Union.

Civil War

In the war that followed, the North won because of its higher population (more than double that of the South) and its vast industrial power. In a process that would be repeated in both the World Wars of the twentieth century, the might of American industry, four-fifths of it located in Northern states, was mobilised to produce huge quantities of armaments and machinery. The primarily agricultural South was blockaded from overseas trade, and by 1864, its economy was broken and its population starving.

Lincoln had gone to war to preserve the Union, not to end slavery. However, as the war went on, events overtook him. Slaves in the South were refusing to obey orders now that their masters were away fighting, and Northern opinion was growing more radical. The great abolitionist Frederick Douglass, himself a former slave, declared: 'Fire must be met with water, darkness with light, and war for the destruction of liberty must be met with war for the destruction of slavery.' In 1863, Lincoln issued the **Emancipation Proclamation**, which ended slavery and made all slaves in America free.

On 9 April 1865, the veteran Southern general Robert E. Lee, commander of the Confederate army, surrendered to the Union in a small Virginian village named Appomattox. After four years of warfare and over 600 000 dead, the United States were reunited. Two days later, Abraham Lincoln was at the theatre when a Southern fanatic named John Wilkes Booth shot and killed him. Lincoln immediately became a martyr for the cause of emancipation and has been honoured by Americans ever since.

The Gettysburg Address

The decisive clash of the American Civil War was the Battle of Gettysburg, fought over several days in July 1863. An estimated 50 000 soldiers were killed or wounded, and it took months to clear the corpses from the battlefield. When a cemetery was finally opened on 19 November, Lincoln attended and gave a short speech. **The Gettysburg Address** became one of the most famous speeches in American history. Lincoln stated that the North was fighting to preserve the true values of the American republic. He promised 'that these dead shall not have died in vain, that this nation under God shall have a new birth of freedom, and that government of the people, by the people, for the people, shall not perish from the earth'.

Check your understanding

1. How was the divide between free and slave-owning states maintained as the United States expanded its territory?
2. What did the Southern states do in response to the election of Abraham Lincoln in 1860?
3. Why did the North win the American Civil War?
4. What was Lincoln's message in the Gettysburg Address?
5. How did the American Civil War bring about the end of slavery in the United States?

Segregation and terror

With slavery abolished, many white Americans sought new ways to deny the black population any real freedom. In the South, they built a social system designed to create a permanent black underclass.

The Jim Crow South

In 1860, there were approximately four million black slaves in America out of a total population of around 31 million. When the war was over, they had their freedom, but they were trapped in a society that was determined to deny them equal rights. The Southern states passed laws that became known as the '**Jim Crow**' **laws**, requiring black Americans to live their lives almost entirely separately from white Americans. This was the system known as **segregation**, meaning the enforced separation of races. It was a legal injustice that would endure for a hundred years.

A segregated waiting area at the Public Health Service Dispensary in Washington, D.C.

In the Jim Crow South, black Americans were forced to attend separate schools, live in separate housing, eat in separate restaurants and even use separate toilets. Black people were required to use separate entrances for public buildings and to sit in separate sections (at the back) on public transport. In theory, all facilities were meant to be 'separate but equal', but in practice this was almost never enforced. Schools for black people were underfunded; housing districts were crowded and poorly built; toilets were squalid. Any black person who attempted to enter a whites-only venue or use facilities for white people would be arrested, probably imprisoned, and very often beaten up by police or white bystanders.

Segregation was upheld by the **Supreme Court** – America's highest legal authority, which holds the power to interpret and enforce American law. When Homer Plessy deliberately sat in a whites-only part of a train in order to test the legal system, the resulting Supreme Court case, *Plessy v. Ferguson* (1896), ruled that segregation was wholly legal. There was nothing black Americans could legally do to overturn the oppressive regime under which they were forced to live.

Who was Jim Crow?

Jim Crow was a character created by a minstrel show actor around 1830. The name became widely used as a derogatory term for black Americans.

Prison labour

The Thirteenth Amendment to the US constitution, which abolished slavery, stated: 'Neither slavery nor involuntary servitude, except as punishment for a crime whereof the party shall have been duly convicted, shall exist within the United States.' The inclusion of the clause on criminal punishment created a loophole, meaning that black people could still be used for slave labour if they were convicted of a crime. Huge numbers of black men were arrested on trumped-up charges and in effect re-enslaved as prisoners. Groups of labouring prisoners called 'chain gangs' became a common sight in the South.

Lynching and terror

In the Jim Crow South, the inferior position of black people was routinely enforced by violence. Black people who did not show the expected level of respect towards white people were **lynched**, meaning murdered by a white mob. Lynchings were common and usually went unpunished.

One organisation in particular made it their goal to terrorise black communities. In 1866, Confederate ex-soldiers in Tennessee founded the **Ku Klux Klan** (from the Greek *kuklos*, meaning 'circle'). The Klan's mission was to enforce white supremacy in America. Wearing white robes and pointed white hoods, and carrying burning crosses, the Klan took the lead in lynching black people across the South. The possibility of black men having sex with white women was a particular obsession, and countless black men were lynched following accusations of rape or of making sexual advances. The Klan also targeted Republican voters and used intimidation to enforce support for the **Democrats**, who were traditionally the party of the South. By the 1920s, the Klan had between two and five million members from all across America – one in six, they claimed, of the eligible white population.

Nocturnal gathering of the Ku Klux Klan, 1921

Fleeing segregation and white violence, black people migrated from the South in vast numbers. In what became known as the 'Great Migration', well over a million left during the 1910s and 1920s, followed by another surge during the Second World War. The large black populations that exist to this day in major Northern cities, such as Chicago, New York and Philadelphia, were founded by these migrants. However, black communities in the North still faced discrimination, forced to live in crowded ghettoes and usually working in only the most menial jobs. After all, despite the differences in their history, many Northerners were every bit as racist as their Southern counterparts.

Emmett Till

In August 1955, black 14-year-old Emmett Till was visiting relatives in rural Mississippi. One day he walked into a grocery store staffed by white 21-year-old Carolyn Bryant. After Emmett left the store, Carolyn told her husband he had flirted with her. Several nights later, her husband and two other men abducted Emmett from his relatives' house, beat him, killed him and dumped his body in a river. Emmett Till's lynching became a national media story, yet the incident was not very different from the thousands of lynchings that regularly took place in America. In 2008, in her old age, Carolyn Bryant admitted that she had made up the accusations.

Emmett Till (1941–1955)

Check your understanding

1. How did the Jim Crow laws create a segregated society in the American South?

2. How was the prison system used to re-enslave black men?

3. What did the Ku Klux Klan do to enforce white supremacy?

4. Why was Emmett Till murdered in August 1955?

5. Why did so many black Americans migrate out of the South between the Civil War and the 1950s?

Unit 5: Civil Rights in America
The Civil Rights Movement

In the 1950s and 1960s, a massive movement by black Americans fought for equal rights. This was the Civil Rights Movement.

Challenging segregation

The National Association for the Advancement of Colored People (NAACP), which was America's leading civil rights group, opened the way by launching a targeted legal challenge to segregation in schools. This led to a Supreme Court case called **Brown v. Board of Education** (1954). Black lawyer Thurgood Marshall successfully argued that separate educational facilities were unavoidably unequal by their very nature, and therefore unconstitutional. The court agreed. However, the judges chose not to demand immediate desegregation, but left it up to state governments – which of course were controlled by white people – to implement the decision at their own pace. The result was that no action was taken.

Rosa Parks sat in a 'whites only' section of a public bus in Montgomery, Alabama

The Montgomery bus boycott

The event that is usually seen as the beginning of the Civil Rights Movement happened on 1 December 1955 in Montgomery, Alabama. Rosa Parks, an experienced black civil rights activist, sat in the 'whites only' part of a bus and refused to give up her seat to a white man. She was arrested. On the day of her trial four days later, the black community in Montgomery started a boycott of all the city buses. The city was filled with black men and women solemnly walking to work, sharing car rides, or if they could not find a way to travel, staying at home and risking their jobs.

At a meeting that same evening, representatives of the local black community formally founded an organisation to fight for social justice. As their leader, they elected a 26-year-old Christian minister named Martin Luther King Jr. With a PhD in theology and great talent as a preacher, King's leadership was characterised by firm moral resolve, inspiring rhetoric and a determined insistence on non-violence. Even when his house was bombed several months into the bus boycott, King always preached forgiveness. As he would declare in 1961: 'Ours is a way out – creative, moral and non-violent. It is not tied to black supremacy or communism but to the plight of the oppressed. It can save the soul of America.'

The **Montgomery bus boycott** was King's, and the black community's, first major success. It lasted for almost a year, until in November 1956 the Supreme Court ruled that segregation on the city's buses was unconstitutional. By now, Martin Luther King was becoming a nationally recognised figure.

Martin Luther King (1929–1968)

The Little Rock schools crisis

In 1957, some schools in the South were finally being desegregated following local campaigns. In the town of Little Rock, Arkansas, nine black students were enrolled in the formerly all-white Little Rock Central High School. When the school year began, however, Arkansas governor Orval Faubus chose to block school **integration** by sending in the Arkansas National Guard (the state-controlled military force). The soldiers were ordered to prevent the black students from entering the school.

Dwight D. Eisenhower, Republican President of the USA from 1953 to 1961, had been reluctant to push for change in the South. He believed that social change must happen naturally in its own time, and that forcing it only leads to chaos and social breakdown. But Eisenhower could not allow a state government to directly defy a Supreme Court order. He nationalised the Arkansas National Guard (placing it under the control of America's **federal government** in Washington, D.C.) and then sent the federal army into Little Rock with orders to protect and escort the black students into the school. Despite constant racial harassment from their white peers, the students stuck out the school year. However, in the following year, Faubus shut down all Little Rock's public schools rather than accept more black students. It took another Supreme Court order to force the schools to reopen.

Civil disobedience

In 1960–61, there was a wave of civil disobedience across the South. The most common tactic was to stage **sit-ins**: black students trained in non-violent protest techniques, often directly inspired by Gandhi's leadership in India, would sit at a whites-only lunch counter in a department store and refuse to move when they were not served. When police arrested them, another wave of students would sit down in their place – and so it went on, no matter how many were arrested. Black men were regularly beaten in prison by white police and guards, but the Civil Rights Movement was turning the act of getting arrested into an act of protest.

Black American musicians

Most of America's distinctive forms of music were invented by black people. Jazz evolved in the 1920s among black musicians in New Orleans, and was popularised by artists such as Louis Armstrong. Rock'n'roll, the style that forms the basis of all modern rock and pop music, was pioneered in the 1950s by black musicians including Chuck Berry and Little Richard. Because they were black, however, they could not become big commercial stars. It was Elvis Presley, a white singer performing rock'n'roll in the style of these black songwriters, who became America's biggest musical celebrity of the twentieth century. Elvis played the key role in popularising the new music around the world.

Chuck Berry (1926–2017)

Check your understanding

1. What was the result of the Supreme Court case *Brown v. Board of Education*?
2. How did Rosa Parks trigger the first major protest of the Civil Rights Movement in December 1955?
3. What kind of leadership did Martin Luther King Jr provide for the Civil Rights Movement?
4. Why was there a crisis over school integration in Little Rock, Arkansas, in 1957?
5. What did President Eisenhower do in response to the Little Rock crisis?

The victories of the 1960s

The Civil Rights Movement reached its climax in the early years of the 1960s, when Martin Luther King and his fellow campaigners succeeded in overthrowing the Jim Crow laws.

The Freedom Riders

In one of the movement's most effective campaigns of civil disobedience, student activists in 1961 began targeting interstate bus and rail transport. Segregation on these services was now illegal, but still enforced in practice. Black and white student activists began travelling on interstate buses, challenging segregated seating in the same way that Rosa Parks had done, and also ignoring segregation rules in toilets and restaurants. Many of the **Freedom Riders**, as they called themselves, were beaten up and some were arrested, but they succeeded in drawing massive media attention to their protest.

From Birmingham to Washington

In 1963, Martin Luther King targeted Birmingham, Alabama, for marches and sit-ins. This was the South's most segregated city and a stronghold of the Ku Klux Klan. King understood that protesting in Birmingham would provoke a violent crackdown, and he chose to lead the movement there because he wished to challenge and expose white supremacy in its most open and undeniable form. King was arrested at a march and imprisoned, but the protests succeeded once again in focusing America's attention on the Civil Rights Movement.

The Birmingham campaign was such a success that King chose to keep the momentum going by leading a march to Washington itself. On 28 August 1963, King stood on the steps of the Lincoln Memorial and addressed a crowd estimated at a quarter of a million people. He made what is perhaps the most famous speech in all of history: 'I have a dream'. 'Now is the time to make real the promises of democracy,' he declared. 'I have a dream that one day down in Alabama, with its vicious racists, ... one day right there in Alabama little black boys and black girls will be able to join hands with little white boys and white girls as sisters and brothers. I have a dream today.'

Police remove demonstrators outside City Hall in Birmingham, Alabama

King's letter from Birmingham City Jail

During his imprisonment, King wrote what became one of the defining statements of his politics, the *Letter from Birmingham City Jail*. In it, he explained how non-violent protest was designed to force white Americans to negotiate: 'It seeks so to dramatise the issue that it can no longer be ignored.' He went on 'My friends, I must say to you that we have not made a single gain in civil rights without determined legal and nonviolent pressure. History is the long and tragic story of the fact that privileged groups seldom give up their privileges voluntarily. ... We know through painful experience that freedom is never voluntarily given by the oppressor; it must be demanded by the oppressed.'

Martin Luther King in Jefferson County Jail in Birmingham, Alabama

That day in Washington is often seen as the high point of the Civil Rights Movement. Bowing to public pressure, President John F. Kennedy prepared a civil rights bill for Congress. Before he could implement it, he was assassinated – shot by a lone gunman on 22 November 1963. But his vice president Lyndon B. Johnson, who now replaced Kennedy, carried the bill forward. On 2 July 1964, the **Civil Rights Act** was passed. It made all forms of segregation and discrimination illegal, in every part of the United States.

The Voting Rights Act

Across the South there remained one other massive legal barrier to racial equality: restrictions on black people's access to voting. It was deliberately made extremely difficult to **register to vote**. Registrar offices were open for only a few days a month, for short periods, so that black Americans were forced to risk their jobs by taking time off work to go through the registration process. This process itself involved highly complex tests, sometimes requiring applicants to know the names of obscure government figures such as the attorney general, or to explain complex congressional procedures. The names of newly registered voters would also be published in local newspapers, exposing them to violence in retaliation.

In 1965, King led a march in Selma, Alabama, to protest against voting restrictions. King, many local teachers who joined the march, and hundreds of their students were all arrested. When King next attempted to lead a long march from Selma to the state capital, Montgomery, local police (many of them on horseback) blocked the bridge out of Selma. When the marchers refused to turn back, the police charged at them, fired tear gas at the crowd and beat up dozens of protesters.

The police violence shocked the nation. President Johnson, responding in outrage, rushed to pass the **Voting Rights Act** in August that year. This law forced states to eliminate barriers to black registration. In Mississippi alone, the proportion of eligible black voters who were registered jumped from under 10 per cent in the early 1960s to over 60 per cent by 1968. This was immensely empowering: when large numbers of black Americans could vote, they could begin electing their own representatives to fight for them.

Martin Luther King at the march on Washington, 1963

The view of over 200 000 marchers along the Capitol at the march on Washington

> ### Check your understanding
>
> 1. Why did Martin Luther King choose Birmingham, Alabama, as the target for one of his major protests?
> 2. What points did King make in his *Letter from Birmingham City Jail*?
> 3. How did President John F. Kennedy respond to the march on Washington of 28 August 1963?
> 4. How were black Americans prevented from registering to vote in most of the South?
> 5. What was the result of the protests in Selma, Alabama, in 1965?

Unit 5: Civil Rights in America
Unfinished struggle

American society had been permanently reshaped, but equality under the law did not automatically mean equality in practice. Racism endured, and the fight for justice was far from over.

A radicalised nation

As the 1960s wore on, the mood in America turned bitter. The Civil Rights Movement did inspire other disadvantaged groups to launch or renew their own struggles for equality, with feminist organisations, native American groups, and the gay rights movement all making demands for social justice. But the visibility and success of black rights activism had provoked an angry racist backlash. In every summer during the mid-1960s, there were violent clashes in cities across America, most of them sparked by incidents of white police brutality. The most serious were the **Watts riots** in Los Angeles in 1965, which lasted for six days and saw looting and burning across nearly 130 square kilometres of the city. Many conservative Americans felt that the society they knew was disintegrating around them.

Focusing all the various strands of protest was America's war in Vietnam (see pages 50–51), which became the dominant political issue of the era. Vietnam created a division in American society between those who supported the war and those who opposed it. Anti-war feeling was strongest among young people and black Americans. In the late 1960s vast crowds of protesters joined peace marches in cities across America.

For younger black Americans, the racism that they still faced on a daily basis caused many to feel that even greater radical change was needed. In both North and South, black people were still systematically discriminated against in jobs and housing. They were denied employment and promotion opportunities, and were sold and rented inferior houses at higher prices. When King turned his attention to these issues, he found that the movement's tried-and-tested tactics did not work in Northern cities, where there was no formal segregation and thus no obvious targets for civil disobedience. A march in Chicago in 1966 to protest against housing inequality produced minimal results.

Black Power

In the mid-1960s, the **Black Power** movement emerged. This was a form of protest that emphasised racial pride, accepted a need for the use of force in black self-defence, and called for black control of resources in black communities. The Black Power protesters worried many white Americans, who feared a slide into violence. When two black US athletes at the 1968 Olympics gave the Black Power salute (a raised fist) in front of a global audience at the medal ceremony, they were condemned by most white Americans and suspended from the US team.

Malcolm X

Malcolm X was a radical civil rights leader who believed that King's non-violent strategy was holding black Americans back. The 'X' in his name symbolised the lost African name taken from his ancestors by slavery. Malcolm X believed that black Americans needed to rise up to create their own society, by force if necessary, and to encourage unity with other black people across the globe. He was assassinated in 1965, but his ideas influenced the Black Power movement and he remains a symbol of black pride.

Malcolm X (1925–1965)

In fact, Black Power protesters never actually resorted to violence, even though they threatened it. The same could not be said of the **Black Panthers**, a militant black liberation group founded in San Francisco in 1966. The Black Panthers combined traditional civil rights activism with Marxism and opposition to American imperialism (as they saw it, the global use of American military and economic power to exploit other nations). They believed in self-defence by violence when necessary, and were involved in frequent clashes with the police. The Black Panthers attracted the attention of the FBI, and they were eliminated by the end of the 1960s.

As American politics grew harsher, Martin Luther King began to voice more radical views. King feared that the Civil Rights Movement had ultimately only benefited middle-class black people, and began to suggest that the American system itself was unjustly and cruelly slanted against the poor of all races. But King would never have the chance to develop these ideas. On 4 April 1968, as he was standing on a hotel balcony in Memphis, Tennessee, a white assassin shot and killed him.

American runners giving the Black Power salute during the Olympic Games, 1968

King's murder shocked and traumatised America. It was widely felt that the assassination symbolised all the many disappointments and failures of the later 1960s. Segregation had been legally dismantled, but little had changed in most black people's experience. In some parts of America, segregation remains very severe, and the work of the Civil Rights Movement remains unfinished to this day.

Nixon's Southern strategy

At the 1968 election, there was a major shift in the American political landscape. White Southerners had traditionally voted Democrat, but now a pair of Democratic presidents, Kennedy and Johnson, had thrown their support behind black civil rights. Richard Nixon, the Republican candidate in 1968, realised that he could win huge numbers of votes by appealing to white Southerners who were disappointed with the Democrats. This '**Southern strategy**' won Nixon the election. From this point onwards, the Republicans would rely on the white South for their core support, while the Democrats were redefined as the party of social progress and civil rights. The two parties had essentially swapped positions.

Check your understanding

1. Why was there an increase in social tension in America in the late 1960s?
2. What made the ideas of Malcolm X different from established civil rights activism?
3. Why was there a scandal when two US athletes gave the Black Power salute at the 1968 Olympics?
4. How did the voting habits of white Southerners change during the 1960s?
5. How were Martin Luther King's political ideas beginning to change in the period before his death?

Unit 5: Civil Rights in America
Knowledge organiser

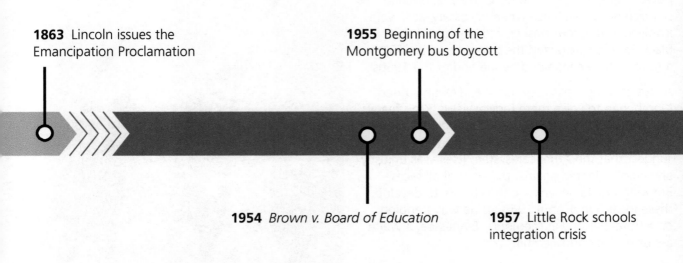

1863 Lincoln issues the Emancipation Proclamation

1955 Beginning of the Montgomery bus boycott

1954 *Brown v. Board of Education*

1957 Little Rock schools integration crisis

Key vocabulary

Black Panthers Militant group that aimed to use force to win more rights for black Americans

Black Power Movement that broke away from the established Civil Rights Movement to emphasise black pride and reject integration

Brown v. Board of Education Supreme Court case that ruled that segregation in schools was unconstitutional

Civil Rights Act Law that made all forms of segregation and discrimination illegal in the USA

Confederacy Confederate States of America; breakaway nation formed by the Southern states of the USA during the American Civil War

Democrats In the USA, political party traditionally representing the white South, later becoming America's major progressive party

Emancipation Proclamation Decree by Abraham Lincoln ending slavery in the USA

Federal government Government of the whole United States, based in Washington, D.C., separate from the governments of individual states

Freedom Riders Campaigners who deliberately violated segregation rules on interstate buses

Gettysburg Address Speech given by Abraham Lincoln when dedicating the cemetery after the Battle of Gettysburg

Integration Process of different groups of people learning to live or work together in a functioning and positive way

Jim Crow laws Laws in Southern states enforcing segregation between white and black Americans

Ku Klux Klan (KKK) White supremacist organisation dedicated to enforcing the dominance of white Americans through violence

Letter from Birmingham City Jail Document written by Martin Luther King Jr outlining his political philosophy

Lynching Murder of a black person by a white mob

Montgomery bus boycott Campaign targeting segregation on city buses in Montgomery, Alabama

Registration to vote Process of enrolment that confirms a citizen's right to vote in elections, required before they can do so

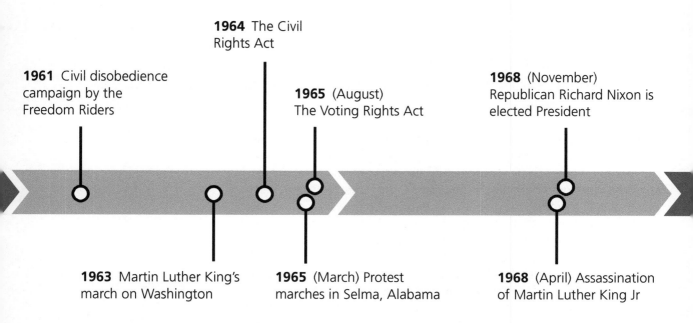

1961 Civil disobedience campaign by the Freedom Riders

1964 The Civil Rights Act

1965 (August) The Voting Rights Act

1968 (November) Republican Richard Nixon is elected President

1963 Martin Luther King's march on Washington

1965 (March) Protest marches in Selma, Alabama

1968 (April) Assassination of Martin Luther King Jr

Republicans In the USA, political party formed to oppose the slave states, later becoming America's major conservative party

Secede Withdraw from a nation or union to become independent

Segregation Forced separation of different ethnic groups in most aspects of life

Sit-ins Civil disobedience tactic in which black people would deliberately sit at a whites-only lunch counter or other segregated area

Southern strategy Electoral strategy of appealing to white Southerners, pioneered by Richard Nixon and adopted by most Republican presidents after him

Supreme Court Highest court of the USA, possessing enormous power to shape American law

Underground Railroad Secret network of abolitionists who aided escaped slaves in the South before the Civil War

Voting Rights Act Law that required all states to remove barriers to black Americans registering to vote

Watts riots Massive race-based riots in Los Angeles in 1965

Key people

Lyndon B. Johnson Democrat President who passed the Civil Rights Act and Voting Rights Act

Martin Luther King Jr Main leader of the Civil Rights Movement, who emphasised non-violent protest

Abraham Lincoln President who governed the North during the American Civil War and issued the Emancipation Proclamation

Thurgood Marshall Black American lawyer who won the *Brown v. Board of Education* case; later the first black judge to sit on the Supreme Court

Richard Nixon President who replaced Lyndon B. Johnson and won support for the Republicans by appealing to white Southerners

Rosa Parks Black activist whose refusal to give up her seat on a city bus began the Montgomery bus boycott

Emmett Till Black teenager lynched in 1955, whose murder became a nationwide scandal

Malcolm X Radical civil rights leader who believed that black Americans needed to create their own independent society, using force if necessary

The origins of the Cold War

For forty-five years after the Second World War, the USA and the USSR confronted each other in a period of rivalry and tension called the Cold War.

Though they had worked together to defeat Nazi Germany, the Americans and the Soviets were deeply ideologically opposed. With the imperial powers of Europe effectively broken by the effort of war, the two **superpowers** now dominated the world – and aimed to exert their power and their influence globally. As the Americans worked to protect capitalism and allied democracies throughout the world, so the Soviets attempted to inspire and direct communist revolution. The USA and the USSR never actively went to war with each other in these years, but they worked against each other in every other possible way, through spying, diplomacy, economics and **proxy wars** (where the USA and USSR supported rival sides in wars involving smaller nations). At frequent moments, the tension between the superpowers became so high that a Third World War could easily have broken out between them. Thankfully, however, the Cold War never turned 'hot'.

The Cold War in Europe

The Cold War split Europe down the middle. In 1944–45, Stalin's Red Army liberated almost the whole of eastern Europe from Nazi domination. Those soldiers did not go home when the war was over. Instead, Stalin took the opportunity to impose communist governments on the nations of eastern Europe: Poland, Hungary, Czechoslovakia, Bulgaria and Romania. Stalin's principal motive was to create a '**buffer zone**' of friendly nations between Russia and Germany, in order to guard against any future German attack.

Between 1945 and 1948, communist parties in these countries, directed from Moscow, used a range of tactics to secure political control. Sometimes there was a direct takeover, such as the coup in February 1948 that brought communists to power in Czechoslovakia. More commonly, elections to form new governments were manipulated by violence, intimidation and fraud in order to produce communist victories. Once control was secure, regimes were established that imitated the systems and techniques of Stalin's USSR. The newly communist states of eastern Europe were theoretically still independent nations, but in practice they became '**satellite states**' of the USSR – smaller, less powerful nations that depended on, and were directed by, the superpower. Eastern Europe had swapped one form of tyranny for another.

NATO

In 1949, the USA and the nations of western Europe formed the **North Atlantic Treaty Organisation (NATO)**, a defensive military alliance that bound them all to defend each other against any external aggression.

Harry S. Truman (1884–1972)

Alarmed by the spread of Soviet power, the Americans resolved to do all they could to prevent communism from spreading any further – a policy known as **containment**. In 1947, President Harry S. Truman declared that America would support any nation under threat from communist revolution or attack. This was known as the **Truman Doctrine**, and it became the basis for American foreign policy throughout the Cold War.

Europe thus became divided into two spheres of influence under the two superpowers. In a speech in March 1946, when many observers already foresaw the complete division of Europe, Winston Churchill declared that 'an **iron curtain** has descended across the continent'. The term 'Iron Curtain' soon became widely used to describe the division between western, American-allied, capitalist Europe and eastern, Soviet-dominated, communist Europe.

Divided Germany

The Iron Curtain also ran right through the heart of the most strategically important nation in Europe: Germany. In 1945, Germany was occupied by the Americans, British and French in the west, and by the Soviets in the east. This division was never intended to be permanent, but it soon became clear that neither side was willing to give up control of their part of the country. Talks aimed at reunification failed because both the Americans and the Soviets feared that a reunited Germany might ally with the other against them. Eventually the Americans decided to establish West Germany as an independent nation. Stalin attempted to prevent this by imposing the **Berlin blockade** (see pages 68–69). When this failed, he had no alternative but to establish East Germany as a separate nation as well.

West Germany emerged as a stable, tolerant and peaceful country, widely regarded as a model of successful capitalist democracy. It also boomed economically, surging ahead in prosperity to overtake the UK as the largest, most dynamic economy in Europe. East Germany, meanwhile, became merely another Soviet satellite state. A communist dictatorship was established, backed by a powerful secret police agency called the **Stasi**. They presided over a country marked by poor living conditions, constant surveillance and censorship, and the imprisonment and torture of those who dared to speak out against the regime.

Marshall Plan

One of the first consequences of the policy of containment was the **Marshall Plan**, a massive programme of financial aid that provided $12.7 billion of American money to help rebuild the nations of western Europe. The Americans feared that the postwar environment of poverty and ruin might cause the people of western Europe to turn to communism, in the same way that the Great Depression had led to the rise of the Nazis. Paying for European reconstruction was seen as better than risking communist revolution in France or Italy.

Check your understanding
1. Why did Stalin impose communist governments on the nations of eastern Europe?
2. What was the policy of containment?
3. What did Churchill mean by the phrase 'Iron Curtain'?
4. Why did the United States provide financial aid to the nations of western Europe?
5. Why did Germany become divided into two separate nations after the Second World War?

Cold War crises

The most dangerous moments in the Cold War were the crises that could have caused it to turn 'hot'. Two of the most serious were the Berlin blockade and the Korean War.

The Berlin blockade

When Germany was occupied in 1945, the city of Berlin lay deep within the Soviet zone. However, because of its political importance, the city was divided just as the German nation was: its western sectors were occupied by the Americans, British and French, while the Soviets controlled the east. The western sectors of Berlin formed a tiny pocket of Western control, over 100 kilometres behind the Iron Curtain. This made them extremely vulnerable to Soviet pressure.

In June 1948, the British, French and Americans introduced a new currency, the Deutschmark, in their zones of Germany – a major step towards creating an independent West German nation. Stalin responded by imposing the Berlin blockade. Road and rail links between West Berlin and the world outside were blocked, electricity was cut off, and all imports of food and fuel were halted. West Berlin in effect became an isolated island, under siege in the middle of Soviet-governed territory.

Map showing divided Germany and divided Berlin

The USA responded to the Berlin blockade by launching the **Berlin airlift**, a programme of supply that brought vital emergency rations to the city by aeroplane. Regular flights were soon bringing thousands of tonnes of supplies to West Berlin every day. At the height of the operation, a plane was landing in Berlin every 90 seconds. This was vastly expensive at a time when Europe was still struggling to feed itself after the war. Yet the Americans were determined to keep West Berlin alive and free. At last, when the airlift had been sustained through the winter, Stalin accepted that his attempt to intimidate the West had failed. The blockade was lifted in May 1949.

The two sides of the Berlin Wall in 1962

The Berlin Wall

Throughout the Cold War, West Berlin survived as a tiny, isolated outpost of West Germany: an island of freedom inside the Soviet empire. For some years it served as an escape route from communism, as East German citizens who wished to flee their repressive government could come to Berlin, cross into the western sector and then take one of the trains that still connected West Berlin with the rest of the free world. By the middle of 1961, almost three million people had fled communism by going through Berlin. The East German authorities could not allow this to continue. On the night of 13 August 1961, they built a wall across Berlin, locking off the western city behind a concrete and barbed wire barrier. The escape route to the West was closed.

The **Berlin Wall** was seen to represent the failure of communism. East Germany could not motivate its people to stay, so it had to stop them leaving by force. The wall also became an internationally recognised symbol of division and repression.

The Korean War

Korea had been ruled by Japan since 1910. When the Japanese surrendered to the Allies in 1945, the country was divided much like Germany, with the USSR controlling the north and the USA controlling the south. Both superpowers withdrew in the late 1940s, but Korea was not reunited. Instead, two separate nations were established, democratic South Korea and communist North Korea.

On 25 June 1950, the dictator of North Korea, Kim Il-sung, launched an invasion of the south. He had Stalin's approval, but only because Stalin assumed that the USA would not intervene. This proved incorrect. North Korea's unprovoked attack caused outrage in Washington, D.C., and President Truman resolved to oppose it. The Americans still had an army occupying Japan, so they were able to quickly send troops to defend South Korea.

At first the American counter-attack was successful, and their armies advanced far into North Korea itself. By October it even looked as though Kim Il-sung's government would have to flee, and Korea might be reunited. Stalin chose not to intervene, unwilling to risk direct war with the USA by sending in Soviet troops. But then a different communist power stepped in to support North Korea: China, which had become a communist nation in 1949. Chinese armies launched a massive counter-attack against the Americans in Korea on 26 November, and began pushing them back southwards.

For almost three more years, American and Chinese armies battled each other across Korea. The combat often resembled the static, trench-based warfare of the First World War, and neither side could secure a definite advantage. When an armistice was agreed in July 1953, the border between North and South Korea ran in roughly the same place that it had done in 1950. That armistice has held ever since, and the two countries are still separated by that same border. North Korea remains a communist dictatorship, and the descendants of Kim Il-sung are still in power. South Korea has remained a democracy.

The Demilitarised Zone (no man's land) between North and South Korea

Check your understanding

1. What prompted Stalin to impose the Berlin blockade in June 1948?

2. How did America respond to the Berlin blockade?

3. Why did the government of East Germany build the Berlin Wall on 13 August 1961?

4. How had two separate Korean nations been established by 1950?

6. How did America and China end up at war against each other in Korea?

Unit 6: The Cold War
Nuclear weapons

When the USA dropped atomic bombs on Hiroshima and Nagasaki in 1945, the world entered the nuclear age. The Cold War was defined by the possibility that these weapons might be used again.

The nuclear threat

The destructive power of nuclear weapons was (and remains) so great that the possibility of their use threatens the continued existence of human civilisation. Not only are nuclear explosions immensely large and destructive blasts, but they also release vast amounts of nuclear radiation, which damages living matter on a molecular level. Living things affected by radiation experience radiation sickness, which can lead to death within hours or even minutes. For those who are not exposed to enough radiation to die immediately, cancers swiftly develop. If for any reason large numbers of nuclear bombs were to be used, most living things on the planet would sicken and die.

Mushroom cloud of the atom bomb over Nagasaki

The USSR developed its own nuclear bomb in 1949. For the duration of the Cold War, the USA and the USSR both stockpiled nuclear weapons and were prepared at any moment to use them against each other. Each of the superpowers possessed the ability to obliterate the other – and indeed to endanger all life on Earth – many times over.

Both the Americans and the Soviets were relying on what is known as the **deterrent** effect. This is the theory that a nation possessing nuclear weapons will never have to use them, because nobody will dare attack it. When both the USA and the USSR were relying on their nuclear arsenals as deterrents, the effect worked both ways. If either of the superpowers used nuclear weapons against the other, the nuclear firepower unleashed by both would be so great that both nations would be wiped out – a situation known as **mutually assured destruction** (shortened to MAD). As a result, in theory, neither country would be willing to 'press the button'.

In practice, we now know that the world came close to near-total destruction several times during the Cold War, as both the Americans and the Soviets came within a whisker of deliberately or accidentally firing nuclear weapons. Probably the most dangerous of these near-misses, and the closest the world has ever come to nuclear war, was the Cuban Missile Crisis of 1962.

The Cuban Missile Crisis

In 1959, a communist revolution led by Fidel Castro took place in the Caribbean island nation of Cuba. The Americans were alarmed by the presence of a communist regime allied to the Soviet Union less than 150 kilometres from the US coastline. In 1961, the USA supported an attempt by CIA-trained Cuban exiles to overthrow Castro's government. This was called the Bay of Pigs invasion.

The leader of the Soviet Union at this time was Nikita Khrushchev, who came to power following the death of Stalin in 1953. In 1962, Khrushchev chose to station Soviet nuclear missiles in Cuba. This was to deter the USA from intervening again, and to provide nuclear protection for future communist revolutions that Khrushchev hoped would take place in Central and South America. By sending missiles to Cuba, Khrushchev was actually placing the two superpowers

Fidel Castro and Nikita Khrushchev together

on a more equal footing, because the USA already had nuclear missiles stationed in Turkey at a comparable distance from the USSR. Nevertheless, when American spy planes detected the missiles in Cuba in October 1962, the news immediately triggered a crisis.

For thirteen days the two superpowers were locked in a deadly stand-off. President John F. Kennedy imposed a naval blockade to prevent any more missiles from reaching Cuba, and demanded that Khrushchev dismantle and remove the missiles that were already there. Khrushchev refused to back down, and the world seemed to be on the brink of nuclear conflict. But at last a deal was struck. Kennedy publicly pledged not to attempt any more invasions of Cuba, and in exchange Khrushchev agreed to withdraw the missiles. Secretly, Kennedy also agreed to remove the US missiles that were stationed in Turkey. The blockade of Cuba was lifted, and the world breathed a sigh of relief.

Recognising how close they had come to nuclear war, after 1962 both the Americans and the Soviets began making certain efforts to decrease tensions and to reduce the risk of conflict. In the later 1960s and 1970s the superpowers entered a period of **détente**, meaning slightly improved relations and limited but important cooperation. In 1972, a series of meetings called the Strategic Arms Limitations Talks led to a treaty called SALT I, which for the first time placed limits on the number of nuclear missiles that each side could possess.

Chernobyl

On 26 April 1986, there was an accidental explosion at the Soviet nuclear power plant at **Chernobyl**, in the Ukraine. It released over a hundred times the radiation of the bombings of Hiroshima and Nagasaki combined. The atomic fallout was carried by the wind over much of Europe. Figures are disputed, but at least 4000 and perhaps closer to 100 000 people are estimated to have died from medical conditions directly linked to Chernobyl.

Check your understanding

1. What makes nuclear weapons so extraordinarily destructive?
2. What is the theory of the nuclear deterrent?
3. Why did Nikita Khrushchev station Soviet nuclear missiles in Cuba in 1962?
4. What agreement did Khrushchev and Kennedy make to resolve the Cuban Missile Crisis?
5. How did the superpowers attempt to limit the risk of nuclear war in the period following the Cuban Missile Crisis?

The collapse of communism

At the end of the 1980s, the USSR and its network of eastern European satellite states rapidly collapsed, and communism all but disappeared from Europe. The Cold War was over.

All this happened without the need for attack or sabotage by the West. Instead, the Soviet system failed on its own. For decades the USSR had been a stagnant society, with an economy that had stopped growing and was only a fraction of the size of the USA's. Few Soviet citizens believed in communism anymore – they simply went through the motions and obeyed their leaders.

In 1985, Mikhail Gorbachev became the Soviet leader. Knowing that the country was failing, he hoped to revive it by launching reforms that would take the USSR in a new direction. Yet the process of change that he began would go further than Gorbachev ever intended, finally resulting in the abolition of the system he hoped to save.

Mikhail Gorbachev (born 1931)

The end of the USSR

Gorbachev had two major new policies: **glasnost** and **perestroika**. *Perestroika* ('restructuring') was an economic policy based on introducing elements of capitalism into the communist system. The other policy, *glasnost* ('openness'), meant that Soviet citizens, including journalists, were now free to access government information, report and discuss it freely, and if they wished, criticise the government.

The effect of *glasnost* was explosive. Soviet media began attacking the government over everything from the apalling state of Soviet housing to the USSR's serious lack of environmental protections. Still hoping that public faith in the system could be restored, Gorbachev took the extraordinary step of allowing non-communist candidates to stand in a nationwide election in 1989. The Communist Party still won the majority of seats, but it now faced open opposition.

Gorbachev was becoming increasingly unpopular with the Soviet people (even though he was admired in the West). This was because *perestroika* had led to food shortages and higher prices, making daily life worse for most ordinary people. In 1990, a prominent critic of Gorbachev named Boris Yeltsin was elected president of Russia (see fact box). Yeltsin argued that Gorbachev's reforms did not go far enough, and called for a full transition to capitalism.

Some of the republics of the Soviet Union were seeking to become separate nations, with Lithuania declaring independence in March 1990. In August 1991, a small group of Communist Party politicians attempted to regain control of the USSR by launching a coup and placing Gorbachev under house arrest. They hoped to reverse Gorbachev's reforms.

The USSR and Russia

The Soviet Union was officially made up of 15 republics. Even though the term 'Soviet Russia' is often used to mean the whole USSR, Russia was technically only one of the republics within it.

Yeltsin spoke out against the coup and inspired massive protests against it, causing it to collapse. He then used his newfound authority to push for the complete separation of all remaining Soviet republics. On 26 December 1991, the Soviet Union was officially dissolved.

Democracy in eastern Europe

While communism was disintegrating in the USSR, pro-democracy movements campaigned for change in the satellite states. Gorbachev signalled in a speech at the United Nations in 1988 that he would not use the Red Army to enforce communism in eastern Europe. The people of the satellite states understood that they were free to go their own way. Many of their leaders, realising that communism was failing, quietly made plans to give up power. In Poland, a free election was scheduled for June 1989.

Boris Yeltsin standing on a tank to address a crowd

The Polish election produced a government headed by **Solidarity**, a trade union turned political party. Solidarity had been formed in 1980, but because communist governments were (in theory) meant to be run by the workers, the existence of an independent workers' union that opposed the government was an embarrassment. Solidarity had been banned and driven underground. Yet now they were in charge of Poland.

The election of Solidarity inspired the people of the other satellite states to reject their communist rulers. Protesters poured onto the streets of Prague and Berlin. Hungary opened its border with democratic Austria, allowing residents of the communist states to pass through Hungary and on into the West. On 9 November 1989, the East German communists announced that they planned to allow free exit into West Berlin. Without waiting for confirmation, massive crowds of Germans in both halves of the city surged towards the Berlin Wall. The border guards laid down their weapons and abandoned their posts. Amid vast celebrations, the people of Berlin tore down the wall.

By the end of 1989, communism had been overthrown in Poland, Hungary, East Germany, Czechoslovakia, Romania and Bulgaria. The transition was almost entirely peaceful: only in Romania did the communists put up violent resistance to their removal, but they were swiftly defeated. In 1990, West and East Germany were officially reunited, becoming a single nation once again. Communism in Europe had disappeared into history.

The fall of the Berlin Wall in 1989

Check your understanding
1. What two new policies did Mikhail Gorbachev introduce in the Soviet Union?
2. Why did Gorbachev become so unpopular with the Soviet people?
3. Why was Boris Yeltsin able to push for the dissolution of the USSR in 1991?
4. Why did the communist nations of eastern Europe all abandon communism in 1989?
5. How did the Berlin Wall come down?

Unit 6: The Cold War
European integration

Throughout the postwar period, Europe moved closer and closer into an international union, designed to foster trade and cooperation between European countries.

The European Coal and Steel Community (ECSC)

After the Second World War, the nations of western Europe needed to rebuild their economies. In 1950, the influential French politician Jean Monnet proposed the **Schuman Plan** (named after France's foreign minister), which led to the creation of the **ECSC**. This was an organisation of six nations: France, West Germany, Italy, Belgium, Luxembourg and the Netherlands. Its purpose was to strengthen the economies of the six nations by managing the production of coal and steel, which were vital industrial resources. The plan was backed by the USA because they believed that European cooperation would form an important safeguard against the threat of communism.

French Foreign Minister Robert Schuman announcing the plan to form the ECSC in front of the national assembly in Paris, 9 May 1950

The European Economic Community (EEC)

In 1957, the **Treaty of Rome** upgraded the ECSC to the **European Economic Community**. This created a 'common market', eliminating tariffs (taxes on imports) so that goods could be traded freely across all six nations. Free trade in goods meant that new jobs were created, incomes rose and prices fell. In the EEC's first decade, trade between member states quadrupled.

Britain first applied to join the EEC in 1961, recognising that as links with the Commonwealth were cut, Europe was becoming increasingly central to British trade. For a long period Britain's application to join was blocked by French President Charles de Gaulle. De Gaulle wanted France to gain status and power by playing the unofficial leadership role within the Community; he knew that if the British joined, they would rival France in shaping EEC policies. Only when de Gaulle was out of power did Britain finally join in 1973, thanks to Prime Minister Edward Heath. The decision was confirmed in a referendum two years later, in which 67 per cent of British voters voted to remain in the EEC.

Other new members followed. Greece entered the Community in 1981. In 1986 Spain and Portugal joined, recently freed from generations of dictatorship (Spain's Francisco Franco died in 1975). These newly democratic southern European nations were significantly poorer and less industrialised than the rest of the EEC, and so they benefited from economic aid provided through the European system. This process would be extended two decades later, when most of the former Soviet satellite states were allowed to 'join Europe' in 2004. For nations still scarred by half a century of totalitarian rule, the support and funding provided by Europe was invaluable.

The European Union (EU)

In 1992, French President François Mitterrand and German Chancellor Helmut Kohl drew up the **Maastricht Treaty**, which officially created the **EU** in 1993. Some European leaders supported this because the reunification of Germany had made them fearful that Germany might again pose a threat to Europe. They felt that if German prosperity depended on cooperation within a larger system, the Germans would have no reason to threaten their neighbours. However, most of Europe's leaders agreed to the creation of the EU because they recognised the benefits that it could bring to their people.

For its citizens, the EU brought freedom to travel, live and work anywhere in the Union. The introduction between 1999 and 2002 of a common currency, the **Euro**, made trade within the Union easier (although not all member states chose to adopt it). The EU did not replace any of the core functions of national governments: it has no army, collects no taxes, and provides no welfare or social services. What it did provide was a framework for international movement, exchange and cooperation. Many of the EU's supporters went further, arguing that by bringing Europeans closer together, the EU had helped to bring peace to a continent historically scarred by war.

The new system, for all the prosperity and opportunity it created, did attract criticism. The EU remained only partially democratic, with most of its leading officials appointed by governments rather than chosen by voters. The policy of free movement aroused opposition among those who saw it as giving up control of national borders. In the twenty-first century, resentment towards the EU's 'democratic deficit' and concern about lack of immigration controls combined to fuel a backlash against the project of European integration. In some member states, '**Eurosceptic**' political parties appeared calling for the EU to be downgraded or even dissolved.

The Eurosceptic movement reached a climax in 2016, when the UK held a referendum on whether to remain in or leave the EU ('**Brexit**'). The vote resulted in 52 per cent of voters choosing to leave, and 48 per cent voting to remain. This made the UK the first-ever member state to vote to leave the European project. The future of Britain's relationship with Europe appeared deeply uncertain.

Pro-EU and anti-Brexit protesters gathered opposite the Houses of Parliament in December 2016

Check your understanding

1. What did Jean Monnet propose with the Schuman Plan in 1950?
2. Why did it take Britain so long to join the European Economic Community (EEC)?
3. How did poorer member states such as Spain, Portugal, and the former communist nations benefit from EEC or EU membership?
4. How was the European Union (EU) established in 1992?
5. What were some of the causes of the Eurosceptic movement that emerged in the early twenty-first century?

Unit 6: The Cold War
Knowledge organiser

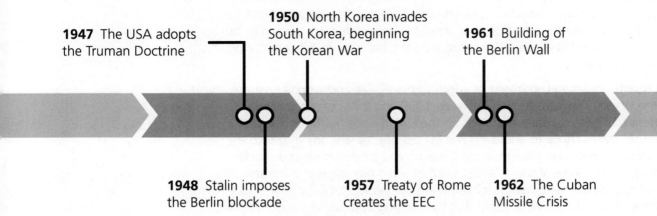

1947 The USA adopts the Truman Doctrine

1950 North Korea invades South Korea, beginning the Korean War

1961 Building of the Berlin Wall

1948 Stalin imposes the Berlin blockade

1957 Treaty of Rome creates the EEC

1962 The Cuban Missile Crisis

Key vocabulary

Berlin airlift Supply operation designed to counter the Berlin blockade by bringing food and fuel rations to West Berlin by aeroplane

Berlin blockade Economic blockade of the Western-controlled zones of Berlin by Stalin in 1948–49

Berlin Wall Wall built by the East German Communists to physically separate West Berlin from East Berlin

Brexit British exit, the departure of the UK from the EU

Buffer zone Territory controlled or influenced by a nation, serving as a barrier to separate it from an enemy

Chernobyl Soviet nuclear power plant where there was a disastrous accidental explosion in 1986

Containment American policy of preventing communism from spreading into new parts of the world

Détente State of improved relations and decreased tensions following a period of rivalry

Deterrent A weapon or threat that discourages people from doing something, even if it is never used

ECSC European Coal and Steel Community, earliest forerunner of the European Union

EEC European Economic Community, economic union of European nations that evolved into the European Union

EU European Union, an economic and political union of European nations

Euro Common currency used by many members of the EU

Eurosceptic Opposed to the EU

Glasnost 'Openness'; Gorbachev's policy of allowing Soviet media and citizens to access government records and freely criticise the government

Iron Curtain The Cold War division between capitalist American-allied western Europe and communist Soviet-controlled eastern Europe

Maastricht Treaty Treaty that upgraded the EEC to the EU

Marshall Plan Massive American financial aid programme that funded the reconstruction of western Europe after the Second World War

Mutually assured destruction Situation in which two superpowers each possess enough nuclear weapons to destroy the other, so any war will result in the defeat of both

NATO North Atlantic Treaty Organisation, a military alliance of the USA with European nations for mutual defence

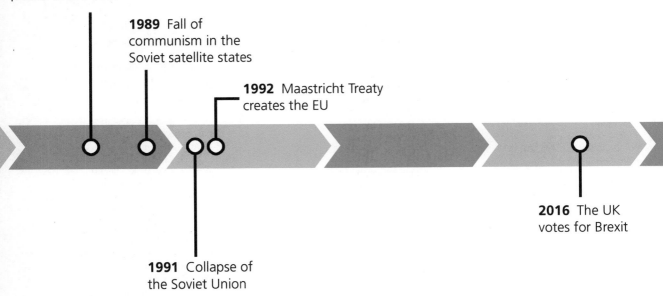

1985 Mikhail Gorbachev comes to power in the USSR

1989 Fall of communism in the Soviet satellite states

1992 Maastricht Treaty creates the EU

1991 Collapse of the Soviet Union

2016 The UK votes for Brexit

Perestroika 'Restructuring'; Gorbachev's policy of introducing elements of capitalism into the communist economy by allowing small independent businesses to form and keep the profits they made

Proxy war Conflict in which two major powers fight each other indirectly by supporting rival sides in a war involving smaller nations

Satellite states Nations that are theoretically independent but in practice controlled by a superpower

Schuman Plan Proposal by Jean Monnet and French Foreign Minister Robert Schuman to create the ECSC

Solidarity Polish workers' union that stood against the Communists as a political party, and formed the first government of post-communist Poland

Stasi The secret police agency in communist East Germany

Superpower Nation with the potential power to dominate the world

Treaty of Rome Treaty that upgraded the ECSC to the EEC

Truman Doctrine American foreign policy to contain communism by intervening to support nations under threat

Key people

Mikhail Gorbachev Soviet leader who oversaw the collapse of communism in Europe

John F. Kennedy President of the USA during the Cuban Missile Crisis

Nikita Khrushchev Soviet leader who stationed nuclear missiles in Cuba, beginning the Cuban Missile Crisis

Kim Il-sung The first dictator of North Korea, who began the Korean War by invading South Korea

Jean Monnet French politician who spearheaded the Schuman Plan, often seen as the originator of European integration

Harry S. Truman President of the USA during the beginning of the Cold War, who established the policy of containment

Boris Yeltsin Russian politician and rival to Gorbachev who pushed for the dissolution of the USSR and then became the first president of post-Soviet Russia

Index

Acknowledgements

I would like to thank my colleague Robert Peal, author of the previous volumes in this series, for very graciously supporting me in contributing a new book to the series he began. My thanks also to the many scholars who have taken the time to read portions of this book and offered invaluable feedback.

Robert Selth

Every effort has been made to trace copyright holders and to obtain their permission for the use of copyright materials. The publishers will gladly receive any information enabling them to rectify any error or omission at the first opportunity.

Text

The publishers wish to thank the following for permission to reproduce copyright material.
An excerpt from 'England Your England' from *The Lion and the Unicorn: Socialism and the English Genius* by George Orwell, copyright © The Estate of Sonia Brownwell Orwell, 1984. Reproduced by permission of Penguin Books Ltd; Quotations on pp.31, 32, 67 reproduced from the speeches, works and writings of Winston S. Churchill, copyright © The Estate of Winston S. Churchill. Reproduced with permission of Curtis Brown, London on behalf of The Estate of Winston S. Churchill; and Quotations on pp.58, 60 by Dr. Martin Luther King, Jr. 24/05/1961, copyright © 1961 Dr. Martin Luther King, Jr. © renewed 1989 Coretta Scott King; Letter from Birmingham City Jail, 16/04/1963, and "I Have a Dream" address, 28/08/1963, copyright © 1963 Dr. Martin Luther King, Jr. © renewed 1991 Coretta Scott King. Reprinted by arrangement with The Heirs to the Estate of Martin Luther King Jr., c/o Writers House as agent for the proprietor New York, NY.

Images

The publishers wish to thank the following for permission to reproduce photographs.
(t = top, c = centre, b = bottom, r = right, l = left)
Cover & p1 TroobaDoor/Shutterstock; p6 Everett Historical/Shutterstock; p8 Pictorial Press Ltd/Alamy Stock Photo; p10 GL Archive/Alamy Stock Photo; p11t Everett Historical/Shutterstock; p11b Everett Historical/Shutterstock; p12t Everett Historical/Shutterstock; p12b Everett Historical/Shutterstock; p14 Chronicle/Alamy Stock Photo; p15 INTERFOTO/Alamy Stock Photo; p18 Everett Historical/Shutterstock; p19 Everett Historical/Shutterstock; p20t Everett Historical/Shutterstock; p20b AF archive/Alamy Stock Photo; p21 Heritage Image Partnership Ltd/Alamy Stock Photo; p22t Everett Historical/Shutterstock; p22b Roman Nerud/Shutterstock; p23 Arterra Picture Library/Alamy Stock Photo; p24t Everett Historical/Shutterstock; p24b World History Archive/Alamy Stock Photo; p26 Granger Historical Picture Archive/Alamy Stock Photo; p27 World History Archive/Alamy Stock Photo; p30 Everett Historical/Shutterstock; p31 akg-images/Alamy Stock Photo; p32t Pictorial Press Ltd/Alamy Stock Photo; p32b Everett Historical/Shutterstock; p33 Shawshots/Alamy Stock Photo; p34 David Ball/Alamy Stock Photo; p35 Pictorial Press Ltd / Alamy Stock Photo; p36 Everett Historical/Shutterstock; p37 Stocktrek Images, Inc/Alamy Stock Photo; p38 Heritage Image Partnership Ltd/Alamy Stock Photo; p39t Everett Historical/Shutterstock; p39b Everett Historical/Shutterstock; p43t Matthew Corrigan/Alamy Stock Photo; p43b UtCon Collection/Alamy Stock Photo; p44 Everett Collection Inc/Alamy Stock Photo; p46t Pictorial Press Ltd/Alamy Stock Photo; p46b Keystone Press/Alamy Stock Photo; p47 Tom Wurl/Shutterstock; p49t Joaquin Ossorio Castillo/Shutterstock; p49b VanderWolf Images/Shutterstock; p50 World History Archive/Alamy Stock Photo; p51 Granger Historical Picture Archive/Alamy Stock Photo; p54t GL Archive/Alamy Stock Photo; p54b Everett Historical/Shutterstock; p56 Everett Historical/Shutterstock; p57t Everett Historical/Shutterstock; p57b Everett Collection Inc/Alamy Stock Photo; p58t Granger Historical Picture Archive/Alamy Stock Photo; p58b Everett Collection Inc/Alamy Stock Photo; p59 Everett Collection Historical/Alamy Stock Photo; p60l Everett Collection Historical/Alamy Stock Photo; p60r Everett Collection Historical/Alamy Stock Photo; p61t Pictorial Press Ltd/Alamy Stock Photo; p61b Everett Historical/Shutterstock; p62 Everett Collection Inc/Alamy Stock Photo; p63 Granger Historical Picture Archive/Alamy Stock Photo; p66 GL Archive/Alamy Stock Photo; p68 Everett Historical/Shutterstock; p69 Joshua Davenport/Shutterstock; p70 Everett Historical/Shutterstock; p71 World History Archive/Alamy Stock Photo; p72 Heide Pinkall/Shutterstock; p73t ITAR-TASS News Agency/Alamy Stock Photo; p73b Agencja Fotograficzna Caro/Alamy Stock Photo; p74 dpa picture alliance/Alamy Stock Photo; p75 Nick Savage/Alamy Stock Photo.